Emotions and Education

Promoting Positive Mental Health in
Students with Learning Disabilities

Nicholas D. Young
Christine N. Michael
Teresa A. Citro

Vernon Series in Education

Copyright © 2018 Vernon Press, an imprint of Vernon Art and Science Inc, on behalf of the author.

All rights reserved. No part of this publication may be reproduced, stored in a retrieval system, or transmitted in any form or by any means, electronic, mechanical, photocopying, recording, or otherwise, without the prior permission of Vernon Art and Science Inc.

www.vernonpress.com

In the Americas:
Vernon Press
1000 N West Street,
Suite 1200, Wilmington,
Delaware 19801
United States

In the rest of the world:
Vernon Press
C/Sancti Espiritu 17,
Malaga, 29006
Spain

Vernon Series in Education

Library of Congress Control Number: 2017956048

ISBN: 978-1-62273-315-6

Product and company names mentioned in this work are the trademarks of their respective owners. While every care has been taken in preparing this work, neither the authors nor Vernon Art and Science Inc. may be held responsible for any loss or damage caused or alleged to be caused directly or indirectly by the information contained in it.

Cover design by Vernon Press, using elements created by Pressfoto - Freepik.com

Table of Contents

Acknowledgement   ix

Preface   xi

Chapter 1   **Everybody Belongs: Structuring Positive Environments**   1

Kristi L. Santi, Jacqueline Hawkins, Caroline Christensen, *University of Houston*

Chapter 2   **Understanding Social Aggression: Bullying and the Student with Learning Disabilities**   15

Linda E. Denault, *Becker College*

Chapter 3   **Learning Disabilities and Anxiety: Understanding and Addressing the Common Occurrence**   33

Nicholas D. Young, *American International College*, and Kristen L. Bonanno-Sotiropoulos, *Bay Path University*

Chapter 4   **Reading, Writing, and Rap: Using Rhyme to Inspire Emotional and Academic Growth**   43

Rosalie Fink, *Lesley University*

Chapter 5   **The Comforting Presence of Visual Literacy Skill in the English Language Arts Classroom**   65

James D. Shivers, *University of Connecticut, The Yale Center for British Art*

| Chapter 6 | **Understanding Student and Teacher Behaviors from Two Perspectives: A Schema for Success in Teaching Students with Learning and Behavioral Challenges** | 85 |

Vance L. Austin, *Manhattanville College*

| Chapter 7 | **Parents Make the Difference: Fostering Emotional Resiliency to Improve School Outcomes** | 107 |

Elizabeth Jean, *Endicott College*
and Nicholas D. Young,
American International College

| Chapter 8 | **Working with Students Who Have Experienced Trauma: Educating Teachers About Trauma-Informed Practice** | 119 |

Micheline Malow, *Manhattanville College*

| Chapter 9 | **Cultural Consideration: Promoting Emotional Well-Being in Students with Learning Disabilities** | 133 |

Nicholas D. Young,
American International College,
Elizabeth Jean, *Endicott College,*
and Anne E. Mead, *Danbury Public Schools*

| Chapter 10 | **Navigating New Turning Points: Transitioning Students with Learning Disabilities to Post-Secondary Promise** | 149 |

Christine N. Michael and Nicholas D. Young,
American International College

About the Primary Authors   175

Acknowledgement

The authors would like to recognize Mrs. Sue Clark for her support and dedication in reviewing this manuscript and providing editorial suggestions. We consider ourselves fortunate to have such a strong ally in the writing process.

Preface

Emotions and Education: Promoting Positive Mental Health in Students with Learning Disabilities was written for practitioners and educators, classroom teachers, staff, and school administrators, as well as parents and students with learning disabilities themselves. This is a book for those who are deeply invested in seeing students with learning disabilities succeed, and succeed at the same rate as their non-disabled peers. While this book largely focuses on understanding the role that emotions and social development play in education, it does so with an acute awareness that these realms may pose unique challenges for children and adolescents with learning disabilities. Much has been written about the academic and cognitive aspects of supporting students with learning disabilities, but few scholars and practitioners have focused their writings on the incredibly important nature of emotional, social, and relational elements of learning.

The motivation for writing this book comes from several concerns:

- *Our belief that all students' socioemotional needs should be at the forefront of teaching and learning;*
- *Our concern about the troubling numbers of students with learning disabilities who are not fulfilling their academic, social, and career potentials;*
- *Our understanding that levels of anxiety, depression, social aggression and other mental health problems are rising, both in society in general, and in our schools, in particular;*
- *Our knowledge that the development of healthy prosocial skills in students with learning disabilities may entail employing different strategies and materials than for non-disabled students;*
- *Our awareness that there are myriad ways in which promoting positive mental health and academic success increase the likelihood that students will thrive in both arenas;*
- *Our years of experience in educating parents, teachers, school counselors, and other helping professionals that has led to the recognition that there is age-specific knowledge*

that could assist these key partners in building resilience and self-advocacy in students with learning disabilities;
- *Our interest in identifying and sharing best practices that lead to academic, personal, mental health, and social success for students with learning disabilities.*

Parents, teachers and others involved in the lives of secondary school students often struggle with the delicate balance of encouraging adolescents to achieve a greater sense of autonomy and independence and inculcating those skills, values and attitudes that they prize before they launch their children into young adulthood. This is no less true of those who support students with learning disabilities, yet the challenges may be even greater, as the support systems so carefully constructed in K-12 settings give way to the greater independence of the college campus. Post-secondary students with learning disabilities may be more reticent to ask for help, and those who care about them may feel less knowledgeable about how to support their academic, career and socioemotional development at this age. This book hopes to provide some suggestions to address these challenges.

Adolescence into young adulthood is a time of many transitions for secondary school students trying to navigate it. By recognizing the nature of this developmental period, educators, caregivers, and other helping professionals can promote pro-social development. Building students' sense of efficacy through improved skills and offering them opportunities to work through developmental issues and personal challenges prior to arriving on the college campus are things that all of us can do. Creating a strong cadre of Students with learning disabilities who can persist to successful college graduation requires school, community, and home commitment.

The concerns noted above are the focal points of the chapters of this book. We have tried to balance theory, research, and data-driven best practice, as we depict the socioemotional and mental health tasks that Students with learning disabilities face and the strategies that may assist them. This book takes a multifaceted approach in that it marries social, emotional, mental health, and transitional components of the K-16 spectrum.

Written by an experienced team of practitioners and scholars, this text attempts to fill the gap in texts that specifically address the needs of Students with learning disabilities in the socioemotional and mental health domains. By providing a foundational understanding of some of the salient issues facing students with learning disabilities, we hope to empower all of those who are working to ensure their success by providing the particular challenges that Students with learning disabilities and their families may face, and strategies and best practices for building creativity, resiliency, prosocial behavior, and positive mental health. As a practitioner and family-oriented text, this book seeks to offer a truncated review of relevant literature followed by suggestions to guide practice.

It is our hope that all who occupy powerful places in the education and development of students with learning disabilities will find valuable strategies to augment their knowledge base, skills, attitudes, and habits. By providing contact information for each of the chapter authors, we wish to encourage readers to reach out to them for further information or to engage in dialogue about what they themselves have found to be successful in their practice.

Chapter 1

Everybody Belongs:
Structuring Positive Environments

Kristi L. Santi, Jacqueline Hawkins,
Caroline Christensen, *University of Houston*

The history of special education legislation can be tied directly to the civil rights movement of the 1960s. During this time, the movement to end discrimination and segregation of any kind helped people with disabilities gain access to both education and work opportunities for which they were previously denied. The disability rights movement secured federal protections with the enactment of the Rehabilitation Act of 1973 whereby the federal government tied the use of federal funds to the recipient's actions regarding discrimination based on disability.

Of particular importance to education was Section 504 of the Act, which contains a broader definition of what constitutes a disability. In 1975, Congress made a more concrete bid to help students with disabilities gain access to the public education system with the passage of The Education for All Handicapped Children Act or PL 94-142. In subsequent revisions, the title was changed to the Individuals with Disabilities Education Act (IDEA) and services were broadened and better defined. While not getting into the legislative process of the laws, it is helpful to provide a quick review of the legislation that has helped pave the way to the concept we present: Everybody belongs!

Current State of the Educational Environment

Students with disabilities have made great strides in general education settings over the past 40 years. Federal statistics show that we continue to move forward as a society with the intent of including all individuals in the general education setting. As evidenced by the fact that in the 2012-13 academic year, almost all students (95%), ages six through 21, served under IDEA – Part B, were educated in general education classrooms for some portion of the academic day.

More encouraging is that more than 60% were specifically being educated inside the general education class at least 80% of the academic day (USDOE, 2015).

Disability rates as a percentage of total enrollment overall remain steady (13.3 in 2000 to 12.9 in 2012); however, there is a shift in the classification category for students. For example, SLD has moved from 45.4 percent of students served in 2000 to 35.4 percent in 2013, whereas autism moved from 1.5 percent to 7.8 percent (Snyder, de Brey, & Dillow, 2016). Thus, while the number of students classified under the Specific Learning Disabilities (SLD) category has a downward trend as a percent of the total school enrollment (6.1 in 2000-01 to 4.6 in 2012-13), this category remains the most prevalent in terms of the percentage of the distribution of students served (45.4% in 1979-80 to 35.4 in 2012-2013) with speech and language impairment second (20.9 to 21.1) (Snyder, deBrey, Dillow, 2016).

SLD is only one of thirteen disability categories under IDEA and we know from the above statistics that students with classifications other than SLD are being educated in the general education classroom setting. SLD, like the other categories, is a heterogeneous group and the 'one-size fits all' approach will not work in any classroom setting. The SLD definition as stated in IDEA as law 20 U.S.C. §1401 [30]. is a disorder in:

> …one or more of the basic psychological processes involved in understanding or in using language, spoken or written, which disorder may manifest itself in the imperfect ability to listen, think, speak, read, write, spell, or do mathematical calculations. Such term includes such conditions as perceptual disabilities, brain injury, minimal brain dysfunction, dyslexia, and developmental aphasia. Such term does not include a learning problem that is primarily the result of visual, hearing, or motor disabilities, of mental retardation, of emotional disturbance, or of environmental, cultural, or economic disadvantage (Great Schools, 2017).

This definition is broad in scope, and to qualify, schools need to have a data-driven approach to show a student's lack of response to evidence-based instruction using a variety of assessment and instructional strategies. Within each category of disability, there is a continuum of ability levels. The range, while typically defined into three categories of mild, moderate, and severe, is a point of reference and not yet one more mechanism to be used as a method of classification. As such, it is not always easy for the general education teacher to develop a comprehensive lesson plan to address all the areas of need for all students in the classroom. The following sections lay out a plan that will help educators to identify student needs, focus on student success, and provide practitioner resources to use in their classroom environments to ensure that all students belong.

Identification and Environment

According to the 2006 IDEA regulations (§300.307) concerning SLD, each state must adopt criteria for determining whether a child has a specific learning disability as defined by §300.8 (c)(10), requiring that states:

- Must not require the use of severe discrepancy between intellectual ability and achievement for determining whether a child has a specific learning disability as defined in §300.8 (c)(10);
- Must permit the use of a process based on the child's response to scientific, research-based intervention; and
- May permit the use of other alternative research-based procedures for determining whether a child has a specific learning disability as defined in §300.8 (c)(10); (IDEA, 20 U.S.C.§ 1414 (b)(6)(A).

Testing. In the United States (US), students with disabilities have historically been identified through the use of the intelligence test, first developed by Alfred Binet in France. This test was revised in 1916 by Lewis Terman of Stanford and is commonly known in the US as the Stanford-Binet (Osgood, 1984). This Intelligence Quotient (IQ) consisted of a single number derived by dividing the tester's mental age by the physical age and multiplying that result by 100. David Wechsler, among others, believed that intelligence involved different mental abilities; consequently, in 1955, he created a new metric test, the Wechsler Adult Intelligence Scale.

From this work, Wechsler developed the Wechsler Intelligence Scale of Children (WISC) and the Wechsler Preschool and Primary Scale of Intelligence (WPPSI). The original model was comprised of two parts, the Verbal Intelligence Quotient and the Performance Intelligence Quotient which combined into a Full-Scale Intelligence Quotient, thus did not rely on a single score. While both tests have gone through many revisions since their inception the basic premise of using the test to show a discrepancy between intelligence and performance is still widely used as a source for the identification of student with disabilities.

The discrepancy model with IQ testing alone is no longer sufficient for identification. In a seminal study on developmental lag versus deficit models for reading disabilities, Francis, Shaywitz, Stuebing, Shaywitz, and Fletcher (1996) investigated the IQ discrepancy theory. In this study, students were classified into three categories (a) deficient reading achievement relative to IQ expectations, (b) deficient reading achievement consistent with IQ expectations, and (c) no reading deficiency. The authors, using traditional definitions, defined developmental lag as the difference in reading ability as compared to cognitive skills development with the expectation that the skills will emerge over time, or more simply put, the students will eventually 'catch up.'

While the deficit model was defined as the assumption that the inability to read proficiently was due to an underdeveloped skill which won't sufficiently develop within that student, the interesting result of the study was the finding that the two groups identified as deficient in reading (a and b above) were not statistically different from one another and that all three groups reached the reading and age plateau at the same age with the groups identified as deficient plateauing at the same level (Francis et al., 1996). While this study was one of many, it was an important step in moving the field into a review of the psychometrics of identification and the need to focus on intervention for all low achievers in all education environments.

Frameworks. With the re-authorization of IDEA in 2004, schools were provided with additional options for identifying students with disabilities. The Response to Intervention (RTI) framework (RTI, n.d.) was one way in which educators could identify students who were struggling by using a data-driven approach. Using a three-tiered model, teachers could document that they were providing high-quality evidenced-based core instruction in the general education setting (Tier 1). Students who did not respond to various portions of the Tier 1 instruction would then receive targeted intervention (Tier 2) in addition to the general education Tier 1 instruction. In Tier 3 instruction, students who did not respond to the Tier 2 targeted intervention received intensive intervention all while maintaining general instruction in the Tier 1 setting. Thus, this instructional framework focuses on the student response to instruction and intervention.

A slightly different instructional framework is the Multi-Tier System of Supports (MTSS) which some refer to as RTI-plus (Metcalf, n.d.). The key differences are the inclusion of social, emotional, and behavioral development throughout the k-12 experience for students in the MTSS framework. Teachers, administrators, specialists, and other district personnel are also part of the equation in that the framework promotes professional development, collaboration, a stronger focus on prevention, and a systems change approach to educating all students. Thus, this model embraces a school-wide systems change approach to the environment to embrace the whole child, furthering the notion that Everybody Belongs.

Finally, the third popular framework outside of IQ testing, is Pattern of Strengths and Weaknesses (PSW). This framework has four features: (a) multiple sources of data using a variety of assessment tools and strategies; (b) use of pattern-seeking techniques for data analysis; (c) predictive and treatment validity; (d) use of logical and empirical evidence to guide decision-making. Thus, the proponents of this model state that a key feature of this framework is the ability of the model to ensure students who are identified with SLD demonstrate one or more processing deficits that interfere with academic achievement (Hale et al., 2010). Thus, like the RtI framework, the focus is on the individual student.

There is much debate around the psychometrics of the models of identification, such as the Response to Intervention, Multi-Tiered Support Systems, the Patterns of Strengths and Weaknesses, along with others (Fletcher et al., 2001; McGill, Styck, Palomares, & Hass, 2016). It is outside the scope of this chapter to discuss the particular issues centered around the psychometric debate. However, practitioners and administrators do need to understand the lack of distinction between students identified and those at-risk of academic failure and the ways in which schools can restructure to make sure the message is clear, both academically and socially: Everybody Belongs.

Student Success

Student success in the public-school setting has focused heavily on the academic side with a more recent push for college and career readiness. Academic success also relies on social skills, self-efficacy, and personal accountability along with cognitive abilities that contribute to the overall academic success of the students. This is important because classrooms are continually becoming more heterogeneous, with the average range of abilities spanning five years, which requires educators to provide a more differentiated approach. In order to ensure differentiated instruction can take place to reach all learners, teachers need routines and structures that promote active engagement within the learning environment. Active engagement is typically only seen as the interaction between the teacher and the higher performing students (Greek, 2000); however, we know the students who need the most assistance often receive the least amount of actively engaged time during the learning day. By matching what we teach to the instructional needs of the students, we actually accelerate the rate of learning and help all students feel a sense of belonging in the classroom.

Academic success

When working with students with disabilities, the areas of deficit tend to be the focal point as it is necessary to help them build skills required for academic success. However, students are better served when teachers approach the instruction with the lens of starting where the students currently are and finding ways to move them to where they need to be for success. Inherent in this approach is a strength perspective that shows how a teacher can leverage students' strengths to build up and/or compensate for the areas of difficulties while promoting student success. Multiple facets are involved in creating environments that promote academic success. This chapter focuses on big-picture ideas, differentiated instruction, and routines.

Consideration. In general, think about the five big picture ideas when planning for academic success.

- Curriculum: How can you adjust the task or assignment so that individual strengths are used to learn new knowledge?

- Pedagogy: In what ways can you alter the presentation of the information so that all individuals can access the content?

- Assessment: When asking students to share their knowledge of what they've learned, how can you work with the student's strengths to ensure that the student can demonstrate the full extent of his/her knowledge without

being constrained by areas of difficulties resulting from the disability?
- Technology: Are there tools available that will assist the student in the learning process?
- Setting/Environment: What are the ways in which the classroom and/or school environment can be altered to reduce disruption in student learning?

Differentiated Instruction includes using data to inform instruction as opposed to a 'plan and teach' only model. This allows for the teacher to target specific skills for small group instruction, in contrast to the one-size fits all framework. Successful differentiation includes:

- Classrooms that are well organized.
- Desks arranged so all students are in the teacher's instructional zone.
- Explicit and systematic instruction – make sure the students know the what and why so there is no guesswork involved in the learning process.
- All students are engaged and are active learners.
- No student is 'written off' as 'that' student' or 'your' student vs. 'my' student.
- Managing classrooms to assure students are working at different levels of knowledge.
- Using flexible groups, moving students around as they master the skills instead of keeping students in the same group based on month or semester.
- Varying the level of complexity of questions and tasks.
- Incorporating routines.
- Creating multi-level activities:
    o Different levels of difficulty and complexity;
    o Step-by-step teaching and learning;
    o Various ways for students to practice learning about the concept;
    o Opportunities for students to show how well they understand the concept.

Academic success is required across content areas and reading ability is the common factor in all areas. When structuring classrooms, teachers must think about the routines and structure from day one of the academic year. This success relies on routines that are consistently followed and understood by the students; successful classrooms have structures in place that run even when a substitute takes over for a day or two. Instructional routines follow a prescribed format but are customized to work within any classroom. This is an integral part of providing differentiated instruction in a meaningful way.

Instructional Routines are conducted in three steps (1) model or demonstration; (2) guided practice; and (3) independent practice. Taking reading as an example, in the first step, model, the teacher demonstrates the skill to be learned by all students in the class using a whole group setting. In the second step, guided practice, the teacher will have the students practice the skill with his/her partner while the teacher walks around checking for understanding. At this point the teacher would start by listening to the students who may be most likely to struggle with reading and take care to ensure the partner is a more able reader. The teacher would come back to the whole group to check that all students have the correct response by using cold calls. In the third step, the teacher would provide students the opportunity for independent practice of the skill while the teacher walks around and monitors performance. While all aspects are essentially the same, some readers may be more familiar with the other names for this routine, "I do, We do, You do" or "Model-Lead-Test."

This is an example of the first day of instruction of a new skill. When teaching a new skill, it is important for teachers to use a short passage that is at the instructional reading level of the lower performing readers. An example of new skill instruction would look like the following:

- Warm-up. When teaching the main idea (also called paragraph shrinking for comprehension) the teacher starts the lesson discussing the objectives for the day. Next, a warm-up activity is used to teach key vocabulary words that will be used in the lesson. The students write one sentence to show their understanding of the words; about one minute per word (with no more than five words used) should be allotted, but this is dependent upon the word choices and the students. Review the definitions with the students and move to explicitly teaching the skill, paragraph shrinking. At this point, students are taught that paragraph shrinking has three main steps (1) identify the who or what a paragraph is mostly about; (2) identify the most important information about the who or what; and (3) shrink all the information into one main-idea statement of 10 words or less (for more on strategy instruction see Honig, Diamond, & Gutlohn, 2012).

- I Do. The teacher reads the first paragraph out loud, using choral reading with the students. Using self-talk, the teacher models finding the three elements of paragraph shrinking so the students can hear the process and understand how some elements are discarded to keep the statement at ten words or less. Incorporating formative assessment (Butler & McMunn, 2006; Frey & Fischer, 2011) throughout the process, the teacher ensures that students are following along with the modeling.

- We Do. The next paragraph is read by the students using partner read aloud and the pairs work together to shrink that paragraph. During this time, the teacher is walking around the classroom to check for understanding and providing immediate feedback. The students can then share their partner work with a neighboring partner group or the teacher can bring everyone back to whole group to check for understanding.

- You Do. The final step is to have all students read the third paragraph independently and complete the paragraph shrinking alone. The teacher still moves around the room to provide immediate support and feedback.

- Exit Slips. Time permitting, the teacher ends the lesson with a check for understanding by having the students summarize the entire passage (remember this was only three paragraphs as the teacher is introducing a new skill, so it wasn't about the article's reading level or length) using ten words or less and handing their work to the teacher as they exit the class. The teacher reviews the work and uses the data to determine which parts of the lesson need to be retaught the next day at the start of the class.

Social Success

A second, essential part of ensuring all students feel like they belong, is the social aspect of the class environment. Students need to be empowered to achieve their goals. Not only do students need to have solid routines in place to serve their academic goals, they have to believe in their own ability to accomplish said goals. They have to believe in their own abilities. Self-efficacy is imperative to academic success and can be taught and promoted by teachers in the types of activities implemented and in the motivation provided. Students must be taught that they can accomplish what they seek to achieve and their efforts must be supported in a nurturing environment.

Self-efficacy. Self-efficacy is what a student perceives about his/her abilities to perform, which does not necessarily reflect the extent of what the individual can do. Individuals prefer tasks that promote confidence and competence and tend to avoid efforts that do not affirm their capabilities (Pajares, 1996). Consequently, it is the responsibility of education to create environments in which students can not only achieve their goals, but believe that their goals are achievable.

According to Klassen and Lynch (2007), "Self-efficacy beliefs influence the level of effort and persistence expended on a task" (p. 494). A number of factors contribute to beliefs of self-efficacy, including past experiences with similar tasks, watching others' performance on similar tasks, the feedback received, and the emotional response to performance and feedback. A student who has previously had a negative experience with a task may avoid that task because they believe they cannot be successful as a result of the factors listed above. Students with LD display lower rates of self-efficacy than their nondisabled peers (Klassen & Lynch, 2007).

Students need to be empowered to achieve their goals. Not only do students need to have solid routines in place to serve their academic goals, they have to believe in their own ability to accomplish said goals. Self-efficacy is imperative to academic success and can be taught and promoted by teachers in the types of activities implemented and in the motivation provided. Students must be taught that they can accomplish what they seek to achieve and their efforts must be supported in a nurturing environment.

Implementing a growth mindset in the classroom can promote self-efficacy. Students need to learn that work takes effort and while they may not always be successful in their endeavors, they must be shown that their efforts are worth the risk of failure because learning occurs with any consequence. Students who are taught a growth mindset are willing to take risks, confront stressful challenges, and continue working towards their goals (Dweck, 2008). A growth mindset teaches students to take responsibility for their learning by teaching them to accept that they are in control of their success and have the ability to counter their fear of failure.

Fear of failure prevents learning by creating aversions to the necessary "experimentation and risk-taking that characterize striving" (Brown, Roediger, & McDaniel, 2014, p.91). Students must learn that their experiences, positive and negative, do not define them, but instead their own efforts allow them to define the experiences and choose how to respond.

Brown et al. (2014, p. 225-228) suggests the following tips for teachers to promote stronger, more durable learning in classroom environments:

- Explain to students how learning works. Students have preconceived, and often incorrect, notions about how they learn. It is essential that they learn that if it feels easy, it probably isn't effective; that, instead, difficulties in learning help them to remember information better. They also need to understand that when they make the effort to learn something new, their brains make new connections, increasing their intellectual ability. The value of failure must also be explained to assure students know that setbacks are acceptable as long as they learn from them.

- Teach Students How to Study. When students are explicitly taught effective study skills and encouraged to use them, they experience their benefits and avoid creating habits of less than optimal methods.

- Create Desirable Difficulties in the Classroom. Spacing, interleaving, and varying classroom topics and problems force students to shift gears and "'reload' what they already know about each topic in order to figure out how the new material relates or differs."

- Be Transparent. Teachers have to explain why they are teaching the strategies and address the concerns and frustrations students may have with the methods. Most importantly, teachers must encourage students to prevail in their efforts and draw attention to students' successes.

Teaching self-efficacy begins with helping students understand how to believe in their own abilities. By teaching growth mindset, educators empower students to see success as a recursive process that is under the students' control. By nurturing a growth mindset in students with LD and without, educators level the playing field by creating a dynamic classroom environment where all students believe they can learn and make the necessary efforts to that aim in whatever academic environment they are employed. Students learn that their social experiences, both positive and negative, do not define them, but instead their own efforts allow them to define their experiences and choose how to respond.

When teachers use these strategies in the classroom, they demonstrate how to master learning. When students accept that failure is part of the process instead of a roadblock, they learn to believe in their own ability to accomplish their goals and become autonomous learners, thinking critically about how to achieve their own goals, and seeking solutions to that end. Ultimately, students who have well-structured, clearly defined routines for learning, a nurturing environment that values differences in a positive way, and a teacher who espouses a growth mindset framework in their daily educational environment, the students will feel like they belong.

Points to Remember

- *Inclusive practices continue to be embraced by the public-school systems.*
- *Frameworks for identification of the students should be viewed as a mechanism for districts to plan for programs and budgets, while quality instruction, research-driven curriculum and intervention should be the focus for all teachers regardless of the framework utilized by the district.*
- *Differentiated instruction promotes academic success of all students. Universal Design for Learning helps promote a socially and academically inclusive environment.*
- *Solid routines help promote a positive class environment where students feel safe and confident in their ability to learn.*
- *Social success, in part, relies on the teacher promoting a growth mindset.*

References

Brown, P.C., Roediger III, H.L., & McDaniel, M.A. (2014). *Make it stick: The science of successful learning.* London, England: Harvard University Press.

Butler, S., & McMunn, N. (2006). *A teacher's guide to classroom assessment: Understanding and using assessment to improve student learning.* San Francisco, CA: Jossey-Bass.

Dweck, C.S. (2006). *Mindset: The new psychology of success.* New York, NY: Ballantine Books.

Francis, D.J., Shaywitz, S.E., Stuebing, K.K., Shaywitz, B.A., & Fletcher, J.M. (1996). Developmental lag versus deficit models of reading disability: A longitudinal, individual growth curves analysis. *Journal of Educational Psychology,* 88(1), 3-17. DOI:10.1037/0022-0663.88.1.3

Frey, N., & Fisher, D. (2011). *Formative assessment action plan: Practical steps to more successful teaching and learning.* Alexandria, VA: Association for Supervision & Curriculum Development (ASCD).

Great Schools. (2017). *IDEA 2004 close up: Evaluation and eligibility for students with learning disabilities.* Retrieved from https://www.greatschools.org/gk/articles/evaluation-and-eligibility-for-specific-learning-disabilities/

Hale, J. B., Alfonso, V., Berninger, B., Bracken, B., Christo, C., Clark, E., . . . Yalof, J., (2010). Critical issues in response-to-intervention, comprehensive evaluation, and specific learning disabilities identification and intervention: An expert white paper consensus. *Learning Disability Quarterly,* 33, 223–236. DOI:10.1177/073194871003300310

Honig, B., Diamond, L., & Gutlohn, L. (2012). *Teaching reading sourcebook* (2nd ed.). Academic Therapy Publications.

Klassen, R. M., & Lynch, S. L. (2007). Self-efficacy from the perspective of adolescents with LD and their specialist teachers. *Journal of Learning Disabilities,* 40(6), 494-507. doi:10.1177/00222194070400060201

McGill, R.J., Styck, K.M., Palomares, R.S., & Hass, M.R. (2016). Critical issues in specific learning disability identification: What we need to know about the PSW model. *Learning Disability Quarterly,* 39(3), 159-170. doi: 10.1177/0731948715618504.

Metcalf, T. (n.d.). *What's your plan? Accurate decision making within a multi-tiered system of Supports: Critical areas in tier 1.* Retrieved from http://www.rtinetwork.org/essential/tieredinstruction/tier1/accurate-decision-making-within-a-multi-tier-system-of-supports-critical-areas-in-tier-1

Osgood, R.L. (1984). Intelligence testing and the field of learning disabilities: A historical and critical perspective. *Learning Disability Quarterly,* 7(4). 343-348. DOI:10.2307/1510234

Pajares, F. (1996). Self-efficacy beliefs in academic settings. *Review of Educational Research,* 66(4), 543-578. doi:10.3102/00346543066004543

RTI. (n.d.). *What is RTI?* Retrieved from http://www.rtinetwork.org/learn/what/whatisrti

Snyder, T.D., de Brey, C., & Dillow, S.A. (2016). *Digest of Education Statistics 2014. (NCES 2016-006). National Center for Education Statistics, Institute of Education Sciences, U.S.*

Department of Education. Washington, DC. Retrieved from: http://nces.ed.gov/pubsearch.

U.S. Department of Education, Office of Special Education and Rehabilitative Services, Office of Special Education Programs. (2015). *37th Annual Report to Congress on the Implementation of the Individuals with Disabilities Education Act, 2015.* Washington, D.C. 2015. Retrieved from: http://www.ed.gov/about/reports/annual/osep.

Chapter 2

Understanding Social Aggression: Bullying and the Student with Learning Disabilities

Linda E. Denault, *Becker College*

Bullying is on the rise. Social aggression, typically the antecedent to bullying, can take many forms, occur in many places, and affect many age groups. Looking back, is there anyone in the adult population who has not experienced, either as a participant or a witness, some form of social aggression/bullying whether in school, in the workplace, or even in the home? Because social aggression appears to be so common in today's society, one might say it is a natural manifestation of the human personality. However, whether always there in the past or more prevalent now, social aggression which rises to the level of bullying has become a problem that can no longer be ignored.

The problem is significant in the 21st century because the Internet has made electronic communication possible for 24 hours each day, introducing the opportunity for cyberbullying. The Center for Disease Control and Prevention (2014) reports that 14.8% of students nationwide have been bullied electronically. Given the prevalence of this issue, the purpose of this chapter is to examine bullying and how it relates specifically to an individual identified as having learning disabilities in order to understand better how to cope with the problem and how to prevent it as well.

Bullying – A Common Practice

Regardless of one's chronological age today, recalling childhood school experiences, one could probably remember incidents of taunting or teasing which occurred, particularly on the playground. The image from old black and white movies of a boy with a "tough guy" stance and an angry expression may come to mind as one envisions the stereotypical bully. However, that typical bully who may have cowered the younger, weaker child is not the only type of individual who may be involved in bullying others. Victims, too, may vary in regard to gender, race, ethnicity, or academic standing. In terms of school-related social aggression, bullying, and cyberbullying in particular, appears to be on the rise.

Bullying in one form or another has been on the school scene for many years; however, bullying has emerged as a more prevalent problem today than in the past due in part to the expanded opportunities for bullying to occur through the 24/7 access afforded by the Internet and various forms of social media. Bullying may be a problem in general to young people of all ages, but it is even a more significant problem for the student with a learning disability. Within the context of a nation seeking greater respect and tolerance in relationships at all levels, this chapter will explore issues associated with bullying and how it can impact the lives of students, particularly those who are dealing with a specific learning disability.

Social Aggression and Relational Aggression vs. Bullying

Social aggression is a term through which we can define the multiple ways in which people react to one another in a hurtful or harmful way within their personal interactions and relationships. Those socially aggressive acts point to single instances or single events in which a person may act out against another, subtly or overtly and either verbally or physically; however, when such acts go beyond solitary incidents and become a pattern of repeated aggressive behavior, they move to another level, becoming bullying, a most notable form of aggression with a distinct negative and potentially dangerous connotation.

Swearer and Hymel (2015) point to the unique nature of bullying, its complexity, and its manifestation in a variety of behavioral patterns and interactions that follow the social-ecological concept of human development (Bronfenbrenner, 1979, as cited in Swearer & Hymel, 2015). As such, bullying behavior can be influenced by multiple factors including but not limited to an individual's personality traits, relationships within the family, school, or community setting, as well as sources of media and technology such as movies, television, video games, and social media outlets (Swearer & Hymel, 2015).

Relational aggression falls under the category of bullying as well; however, it differs in that it is not overt, but more subtle in nature and may be harder to detect (The Ophelia Project, n.d.). These subtle acts of aggression may take the form of gossiping or spreading rumors which can be equally hurtful and have similar negative effects on victims but are less overt.

Bullying Defined

Bullying itself can take several forms and can take place in a variety of settings, with individuals even assuming different roles at different times, ranging from being the bully to the victim to the bystander (Swearer & Hymel, 2015). Although statistics from the U.S. Department of Health and Human Services (Gladden, Vivolo-Kantor, Hamburger, & Lumpkin, 2014) show a high number of bullying incidents take place in the schools (70.6% of students report seeing bullying in school), with the largest percentage of occurrences in the middle school to freshman in high school age range, bullying can occur in or away from school and at all school ages. Yet, as self-reporting surveys show, there were 28% of students in grades 6-12 who reported experiencing bullying at school (Gladden et al., 2014).

Bullying is a deliberate act of aggression and, as defined by the American Academy of Child and Adolescent Psychiatry (AACAP) (2014), involves repeatedly exposing the victim to a variety of physical or relational acts of aggression ranging from teasing to name calling to threatening to taunting to deliberate exclusion to tripping, hitting, or punching. AACAP (2014) reports further that this common problem of bullying is so prevalent that studies have shown one in four students report social exclusion with one in ten reporting being physically bullied.

Demaray and Malecki (2003) concur that bullying is widespread, although the descriptive analyses of their data revealed that verbal bullying, delivered both directly and indirectly, as through name calling or mean gossiping, far exceeded any severe physical bullying.

Similar to the definitions provided thus far, Englander (2017) describes bullying as being calculated, ongoing, and aimed at those perceived to be less powerful; "using this definition, between a quarter and a third of children report being targeted by bullies in a given year" (p. 25).

Rodkin (2011) notes that bullying involves coercive power exerted within the context of a perceived sense of inequality and unfairness where the victims are not likely to retaliate and the abuse is accepted by the peer group, often going unnoticed or ignored even by responsible adults who may witness it or know of its existence. Ross (2003, as cited by Carter & Spencer, 2006) also focuses on the imbalance of power as he defines bullying, further stressing the intentional aspect of bullying which for the most part is unprovoked and repeated over time.

Longevity of the Bullying Issue

This problem of bullying is not new to society nor exclusive to the United States, as other countries have conducted research into the social problem of bullying as well. As Carter and Spencer (2006) point out, reference to bullying behaviors can be found in classic literature; it is not just a "typical childhood experience or rite of passage" (p.11), but a serious social problem that recently has garnered greater scrutiny internationally. Given the increased time that young people spend in a virtual environment, a Korean study by Yang et al. (2006) recognized the growing concern with cyberbullying. Studying 1,344 children of school age and examining multiple factors, Yang et al. (2006) found, among a variety of results, that both bullies and victims engaged in cyberbullying activities displayed lower academic achievement as well as lower self-esteem.

In the United States, the problem of bullying, both traditional (in person) and cyber, is regarded with sufficient seriousness that a White House Conference devoted to bullying prevention occurred on March 10, 2011, aimed at developing strategies to reduce and end bullying in schools (Rodkin, 2011). Bullying warrants national attention due to the dire consequences, up to and including suicide, it may have if allowed to go unaddressed and unchecked. Psychology Today (2017) describes bullying as a durable style of behavior, underscoring a sense of urgency in recognizing the serious nature of this national problem, especially in light of social media opening new avenues for the bully to harass his/her victims.

Farmer et al. (as cited in Rodkin, 2011) look at the bully and see him/her as one who operates within either of two worlds; the bully may be reacting to social marginalization where the bully is not included so acts out or is well connected and exerts power through his/her popularity. Particularly, in terms of the socially connected bullying, the target is most likely to be those individuals who are usually not defended by their peers. As further reported by the American Academy of Child and Adolescent Psychiatry, there are certain groups of young people who are likely victims of bullying; these vulnerabilities are based on factors such as disabilities (physical and/or mental), physical appearance, race, ethnicity, sexual orientation, economic status, and religion. Such factors may cut across age and gender.

Characteristics of Students with Learning Disabilities

Given that young people with disabilities present in a variety of ways and are a prime target for the bully, it is important to identify clearly the student with a disability who is being addressed here; that student is one with a specific learning disability. Special education laws provide a detailed description of that student and how that student's needs are to be addressed in a school setting. Under the federal statute (34 C.F.R., §§300.7 and 300.541), a specific learning disability

> ...is a disorder in one or more basic psychological processes involved in understanding or using language, spoken or written, that may manifest itself in an imperfect ability to listen, speak, read, write, spell, or to do mathematical calculations, including conditions such as perceptual disabilities, brain injury, minimal brain dysfunction, dyslexia, and developmental aphasia. The term does not include problems primarily the result of visual, hearing or motor disabilities, mental retardation, emotional disturbance, or environmental, cultural, or economic disadvantage.
>
> (Massachusetts Department of Education, n.d.)

It is "imperfections" such as these upon which the bully will focus in much the same way that an animal predator will single out its prey from a large herd.

Although providing details of how one is identified as having a specific learning disability, the federal definition provided is relatively broad and would encompass children with a range of issues which might set them apart both academically and socially from their peers. It is these differences in processes, including appropriate application of socialization skills, which makes the student with learning disabilities more vulnerable to ridicule and/or isolation. The research regarding the potential link between bullying behaviors and students with identified learning disabilities is limited; however, a few studies point to a possible relationship between the two. One quantitative synthesis of a meta-analysis of 152 studies examining the possible connection between social skill deficits and learning disabilities showed that 75 percent of students displayed deficits in their social skills as compared to their nondisabled peers (Kavale & Forness, 1996), illustrating the potential for a majority of Students with learning disabilities to become victims of bullying.

Carter and Spencer (2006) examined eleven studies from 1989 to 2003, categorizing students with disabilities by visible and non-visible disabilities. Their work showed that both categories of disabled students experienced more incidents of bullying than did their non-disabled counterparts. The work with middle school-aged students of Carlson, Flannery, and Kral through the University of Wisconsin (2005) also showed that Students with learning disabilities self-reported a significantly greater number of incidents of being bullied than did their non-disabled peers. This study further suggested that a factor in the greater number of incidences of bullying was linked to the Students with learning disabilities having fewer friends at school.

Another study with a similar finding was that of Twyman et al. (2010) who also reported that children with learning disabilities have a greater risk of becoming victims of bullying. Further, Twyman et al. (2010) also reported that the LD child is not only prone to becoming a victim of his/her peers, but is also more likely to become a bully, thus "turning the tables," the antithesis of a desired outcome.

Similar problems with bullying issues plague students identified with other diagnoses which may require educational and/or social intervention. For example, Sciberras, Ohan, and Anderson (2011) found that adolescent girls with attention deficit/hyperactivity disorder (ADHD) were more socially impaired than their non-ADHD counterparts. In terms of both overt (physical acts such as kicking) and relational interactions (verbal acts such as taunting and teasing), the girls with ADHD experienced higher rates of victimization, a pattern which could continue into adulthood. This example underscores the widespread nature of the bullying issue and the need to address it not only for Students with learning disabilities, but for students with other special needs which may set them apart as different from their peers.

The Role of Inclusion

The delivery of special education services appears to play a major role in the dynamics of bullying. Since the late 1980s and the early 1990s, there has been a conscious effort to include students in regular classrooms where they would be educated alongside their general education peers as opposed to receiving instruction in substantially separate classrooms where students would be educated with only other students identified with special learning needs. Inherently, the structure of this model creates a situation in which not only academic but social exclusion as well can occur as a natural yet unintended consequence.

Under the law, the Individuals with Disabilities Act (IDEA), which was first enacted in 1975 as the Education of the Handicapped Act and reauthorized and amended several times since, all public schools within the United States are required to provide a free and appropriate education within the least restrictive environment (LRE) for every eligible child (United States Department of Education); thus, the requirement for LRE gradually led to more inclusive classrooms, especially for students with mild learning disabilities. True inclusion, however, should not mean just in the classroom (where instruction is still provided in a separate setting within the room and possibly delivered by a teaching assistant with materials that may or may not relate to the curriculum followed by the rest of the class), but should mean included as an equal participant in the learning activities planned for all students. In spite of the potential positive outcomes of the inclusive model, a study by Luciano & Savage (2007) suggests that bullying of students with LD may still occur in an inclusive setting with any peer rejection of these students likely being rooted in their language difficulties.

Impact of Brain Research

Recent developments in brain research are making the possibility of serving the needs of all students within the regular classroom, including those with learning disabilities, more possible. According to Willis (2007), contemporary brain-based research provides teachers with a variety of strategies for meeting the needs of individual students, making project-based, cooperative learning more possible and productive, a process which can also lead to changing students' attitudes toward one another, becoming more accepting and positive. Such a basis for students to understand and respect that each person brings different ideas, talents, perspectives, and skills to classroom tasks has the potential to reduce bullying among those classmates.

Students are not as likely to be victims of bullying at school when they are seen in a more positive light by their classmates (Swearer, Espelage, Vaillancourt & Hymel, 2010, as cited in Armstrong, 2017). Speaking from experience as a school administrator, this writer can attest to the change made in creating a more positive and welcoming school climate when inclusion becomes the rule rather than the exception.

Neurodiversity

Academically and socially, Armstrong (2017) concurs with Willis (2007) on the importance of incorporating the most current brain-based research into teaching strategies in order to benefit all students within an inclusive environment and create a positive learning situation. Rather than approaching instruction from a deficit model and attempting to fill in gaps in a student's learning, Armstrong (2017) advocates for a neurodiversity-based approach, tracing its roots back to social and ecological theory, to focus on the strengths of each student in order to enhance skills. For the student with learning disabilities, who often feels inadequate to meet academic expectations in the classroom, a neurodiversity-based approach can reinforce that he/she too is a capable person who can be academically successful (Armstrong, 2017).

Using a difference rather than deficit model will require teachers to make a paradigm shift in their expectations of themselves and of the students with learning disabilities who will be included in their classrooms. If this paradigm shift from a deficit to a different model is made successfully, special education would be more well aligned with the societal emphasis on diversity here in the 21st century (Armstrong, 2017). However, making a paradigm shift such as recommended by Armstrong likely will be a long, slow process, as systemic change of that magnitude is necessarily gradual (Evans, 2001).

A qualitative study by Lynch (2007) indicates one reason why this paradigm shift in the delivery of special education may be slow in coming but also why making the shift is so important. In his study focusing on students with learning disabilities, Lynch sought the perspectives of both students and teachers with regard to self-efficacy. The students with learning disabilities were low in self-efficacy which they attributed to a lack of effort; however, their teachers attributed the students' low self-efficacy to skill deficits, underscoring Armstrong's (2017) point regarding a deficit model and the need for teachers to adopt a different viewpoint and different strategies in approaching instruction for students with learning disabilities.

Cyberbullying

Beyond the structure of classroom instruction, a significant factor in our modern world, which impacts students' lives on a daily basis, is their ability to communicate directly with each other 24/7. Through cellular phones and/or computers, students have access to the Internet and a wide variety of social media sites through which they can send or post messages and photos, often even anonymously, creating an avenue for bullying to occur well beyond the classroom or any other place or event associated with school. The anonymity often afforded the cyberbully also may hold him/her unaccountable. Should an incident of traditional bullying (face to face) occur within the school day, cyberbullying can provide the means by which the bully can continue the aggression, essentially following his/her victim home from school; thus, the victim cannot escape from this harassment even in what should be the safety of his/her home.

For children of today, there is a blending of these two key environments. In terms of communication for school-age children, there is no distinction between the school classroom or playground and private places at home as they remain digitally connected to others; from the perspective of young people, texting is just talking and the Internet offers just another place to be with friends (Englander, 2017).

Impact of Bullying

Simply stated, there are no positive outcomes resulting from bullying. Regardless of the circumstances for the person(s) involved, including issues related to personality, behavior, and/or academic standing, bullying can impact the victim's life in multiple ways, including his/her learning, self-esteem, self-confidence, and social interactions and relationships (Understood, n.d.). The same factors that may cause students to be more susceptible to being bullied may have other negative consequences as well. In terms of academics, students with learning disabilities often experience social anxiety as they may lack the social skills that are necessary for them to feel confident within an educational setting; this level of apprehension can then become a barrier to learning of which teachers need to be aware (Understood, n.d.).

Beyond academics, negative consequences of bullying, when not confronted and addressed, can be significant and even devastating on a social-emotional level. However, monitoring and addressing issues of cyberbullying present a significant yet high-stakes challenge for teachers, school administrators, and parents. The dire consequences of the relentless and public, though often anonymous, nature of cyberbullying is illustrated best through the stories of young people who have tried unsuccessfully to cope with instances of cyberbullying, which can be relentless. The story of Megan Meier provides such an example of online cruelty and the tragic ending bullying can have (YouTube, 2013).

Megan's Story

Megan, who resided in suburban St. Louis, Missouri, was a child who had what her parents described as a challenging elementary school experience due to some special need issues. Starting in a new school as a thirteen-year-old eighth grader, Meg had a fresh start and as part of this new beginning broke off a friendship with a girl in her neighborhood. Shortly thereafter, Meg began an online friendship with a boy named Joshua who had contacted her on social media, professing friendship and offering her many flattering comments. However, this virtual friendship abruptly ended just prior to Meg's fourteenth birthday when Joshua sent hurtful messages, including a statement that the world would be better off without Megan in it. Devastated by these sudden, hurtful remarks, subsequently, Megan hung herself in her bedroom closet. An investigation followed, leading to charges against the mother of the neighborhood girl who was responsible for creating the fictitious account in the name of a boy who did not exist. The neighborhood mother's reason for establishing a fake account and deceiving Megan online was to retaliate for Meg ending the girls' friendship.

Coping with Bullying

Ultimately, it is the individual student who must react to a bullying situation, whether as the bully, the victim or the bystander. Anti-bullying programs offer many suggestions to prevent as well as to help reduce and/or eliminate bullying. Their messages are similar in that they encourage the building of positive relationships and not ignoring bullying behaviors, particularly encouraging the bystander to step up in defense of the bully's target (Coloroso, 2009). This type of intervention is important as it is recommended to intervene within ten seconds of the initiation of an act of bullying to provide a strong chance that the incident will be derailed (Englander, 2017).

For the victim, Coloroso (2009) offers what she considers to be "powerful antidotes" to bullying: having a strong feeling of self-worth, having a good friend, being a good friend, and being able to join a group; these are all suggestions that would contribute to a sense of belonging often absent in students with learning disabilities who may tend to feel as if they were not a part of the regular classroom.

Legislative Response to Bullying

The legislature in the Commonwealth of Massachusetts recognized the seriousness of the issue of bullying and how school-age bullies target the more vulnerable among their peers. In part in response to the deaths of teenagers by suicide within the Commonwealth, a general law was passed to address bullying, requiring schools to establish bullying prevention programs and track incidents of bullying within the schools.

According to MA G.L., Chapter 86 of the Acts of 2014, which amended G.L. c. 71, §370, the anti-bullying statute, and was signed into law on April 24, 2014. G.L. c. 71, §370, as amended, requires school districts, charter schools, approved private day or residential schools, and collaborative schools to "recognize" in their bullying prevention and intervention plans that certain enumerated categories of students may be more vulnerable to being targets of bullying based on actual or perceived differentiating characteristics. Districts and schools must also include the specific steps they will take to support these vulnerable students and provide all students the skills, knowledge and strategies they need to prevent or respond to bullying or harassment (Commonwealth of Massachusetts, n.d.)

Responses at School

Beyond the law, there are concrete suggestions that can be carried out on a daily basis both in school and at home. In school, administrators and teachers must be vigilant and responsive to overt or suspected bullying. "Things often got worse when adults ignored what was going on, told bullied youth to stop tattling, or told them to solve the problem themselves" (Davis & Nixon, 2011, p. 21).

Rodkin (2011) makes several specific suggestions for teachers including: talk with students about bullying; pay attention to relationships and support students who appear to have no friends; ensure that the classroom is democratic and offers a sense of community; use anti-bullying programs/curricula; include a social-emotional curriculum. When talking with students, Twyman et al. (2010) recommend asking Students with learning disabilities directly about any incidents of bullying and any feelings of ostracism they may have, as feelings of exclusion can undermine a child's sense of worthiness, self-control, and belonging.

Englander (2017) points to the importance of teachers recognizing and responding to "gateway behaviors" (p. 27) with an emphasis on the negative impact such behavior has on the entire school community. These gateway behaviors do not break school rules, but include actions which are hurtful such as eye rolling, making rude remarks, laughing, or pointing fingers. When teachers follow the advice given here, the classroom climate should benefit, making it a safer learning environment for all students, including those with learning disabilities.

Voices of the Students

Through a Youth Voice research project, Davis and Nixon (2011) surveyed students in grades 5-12 to gain their perspective on giving advice to victims of bullying. The summary of key student responses, for which students found their strategies effective included: pretended it doesn't bother me (73%); told a friend (67%); told the bully to stop (66%); walked away (66%); reminded myself what they are doing is not my fault and that they are the ones doing something wrong (58%); told an adult at home (49%).

The survey also sought information from students as to how adults were most helpful to them in situations of bullying. Major responses from students indicated that a willingness to listen was critical as was checking later to see if the student was doing well and watching to see that others didn't bother the student who was victimized; such positive relationships with teachers as these findings indicate help build student resiliency (Davis & Nixon, 2011).

The survey also sought information from the students' perspective regarding their perception of how their peers could help in bullying situations. As anticipated, victims of bullying found support and a feeling of safety in friends who listened, who literally stood by them and helped them, and who encouraged them not to listen to the bully (Davis & Nixon, 2011). Being connected to friends and trusted adults at school provides a needed sense of belonging necessary for success for all students and emphasizes once again the importance of relationships.

Conclusion

As pointed out in its 2014 status report, *Bullying in U.S. Schools* (Olweus, 2015), despite serious efforts to increase public awareness, to enact legislation to curb bullying, and to institute programs and support services for children and families dealing with incidents of bullying, bullying remains a serious problem that impacts the entire population of schools in general and the more vulnerable including those students with learning disabilities, in particular. Therefore, given the limited research to date on this topic and the potential it has for dire and irreversible consequences, it is imperative that the topic of bullying, particularly regarding its impact on students with identified learning disabilities, be researched in greater depth and that any recommendations from those studies be shared widely within the general school community and beyond.

Until there are more solutions identified to solve the complex problem of bullying here in the 21st century, it is incumbent upon educators to stay abreast of brain-based research which may hold some answers to approaching learning, especially for the student with learning disabilities, in a manner that builds on students' strengths while at the same time building a more positive classroom environment. With a classroom environment that is conducive not only for academic learning but for positive socialization as well, the potential exists to reduce incidents of social aggression and bullying, many of which target students with special needs.

Given this long-term goal, it is also incumbent upon every person within the school community interested in alleviating this problem to do his/her part to follow the "Golden Rule" and model the respect, civility, and tolerance that could lay the proper foundation for making bullying a thing of the past.

Points to Remember

- *Bullying is a serious issue that is on the rise, boosted by the ease with which young people can communicate digitally. Bullying is a problem for all students, but with potentially more adverse consequences for the student with learning disabilities.*

- *Children with identified learning disabilities are at higher risk for victimization in bullying situations as they already see themselves as different.*

- *Being bullied leads to low self-esteem, feelings of worthlessness, and even hopelessness, with the young adolescent at the greatest risk for bullying. Resulting isolation can have negative outcomes, including life-threatening consequences.*

- *Trusted relationships with adults as well as peers at both home and at school are the key to building resilience.*

- *Based on current brain research, teachers have an opportunity to make a paradigm shift to neurodiversity in the delivery of instruction for students with learning disabilities; a shift of this nature holds the potential for academic and social success.*

References

American Academy of Child and Adolescent Psychiatry. (n.d.). *Bullying Resource Center.* Retrieved from http://www.aacap.org/AACAP/Families_and_Youth/Resource_Centers/Bullying_Resource_Center/Home.aspx

Armstrong, T. (2017). Neurodiversity: The future of special education. *Educational Leadership,* 74(7), 10-16. Retrieved from https://eric.ed.gov/?id=EJ1138105

Bender, W.N., Rosenkrans, C.B., & Crane, M.K. (1999). Stress, depression and suicide among students with learning disabilities: Assessing the risk. *Learning Disabilities Quarterly,* 22(2), 143-156. DOI:10.2307/1511272

Carlson, E.J., Flannery, M.C., & Kral, M.S. (n.d.) *Differences in bully/victim problems between early adolescents with learning disabilities and their no-disabled peers.* River Falls: University of Wisconsin.

Carter, B.B. & Spencer, V.G. (2006). The fear factor: Bullying and students with disabilities. *International Journal of Special Education,* 21(1), 11-23. Retrieved from https://www.researchgate.net/publication/285526605_The_fear_factor_Bullying_and_students_with_disabilities

Centers for Disease Control and Prevention. (2014). Youth risk behavior surveillance – United States, 2014. *Morbidity and Mortality Weekly Report,* 63(4). Retrieved from: https://www.cdc.gov/mmwr/pdf/ss/ss6304.pdf?utm-source=rss&utm-medium=rss&utm-campaign=youth-risk-behavior-surveillance-united-states-2013-pdf

Coloroso, B. (2009). *The bully, the bullied, and the bystander.* Littleton, Colorado: Kids Are Worth It! Inc.

Commonwealth of Massachusetts. (n.d.) Retrieved from https://malegislature.gov/Laws/SessionLaws/Acts/2014/Chapter86

Cowie, H. & Colliety, P. (2016). Who cares about bullies? *Pastoral Care in Education,* 34(1), 24-33. DOI:10.1080/02643944.2015.1119880

Davis, S. & Nixon, C. (2011). What students say about bullying. *Educational Leadership,* 69(1), 18-33. Retrieved from https://eric.ed.gov/?id=EJ963515

Demaray, M.K. & Malecki, C.K. (2003). Perceptions of the frequency and importance of social support by students classified as victims, bullies, and bully/victims in an urban middle school. *School Psychology Review,* 32(3), 471-489. Retrieved from https://eric.ed.gov/?id=EJ823567

Englander, E.K. (2017). Understanding bullying behavior: What educators should know and can do. *American Educator,* 40(4), 24-29. Retrieved from https://eric.ed.gov/?id=EJ1123847

Evans, R. (2001). *The human side of change: Reform, resistance, and the real-life problems of innovation.* San Francisco, CA: Jossey Bass.

Gladden, R.M., Vivolo-Kantor, A.M., Hamburger, M.E., & Lumpkin, C.D. (2014). *Bullying surveillance among youths: Uniform definitions for health and recommended data elements.* Retrieved from https://www.cdc.gov/violenceprevention/pdf/bullying-definitions-final-a.pdf

Houbre, E. Tarquinio, C., Thuillier, I., & Hergott, E. (2006). Bullying among students and its consequences on health. *European Journal of Psychology of Education,* 21(2), 183-208. DOI:10.1007/BF03173576

Kavale, K.A. & Forness, S.R. (1996). Social skill deficits and learning disabilities: A meta-analysis. *Journal of Learning Disabilities,* 29(3), 226-237. DOI:0.1177/002221949602900301

Luciano, S. & Savage, R.S. (2007). Bullying risk in children with learning disabilities. *Canadian Journal of School Psychology,* 22(1), 14-31. DOI:10.1177/0829573507301039

Lynch, S.L. & Klassen, R.M. (2007). Self-efficacy form the perspective of adolescents with learning disabilities and their specialist teachers. *Journal of Learning Disabilities,* 40(6), 494-507. DOI:10.1177/00222194070400060201

Massachusetts Department of Elementary and Secondary Education. (n.d.) Retrieved from www.doe.mass.edu/sped/definitions.html

Olweus Bullying Prevention Program. (2015). Bullying in U.S. schools: 2014 Status report. Hazelden Betty Ford Foundation. Retrieved from https://www.hazelden.org/web/public/document/obppbullyingtrends_2014_final.pdf

Ophelia Project. (2012). *Relational aggression overview.* Retrieved from http://www.opheliaporject.org/ra.hmtl

Psychology Today. (2017). Bullying. Retrieved from https://www.psychologytoday.com/basics/bullying

Rodkin, P.C. (2011). Bullying and the power of peers. *Educational Leadership,* 69(1), 10-16. Retrieved from https://eric.ed.gov/?id=EJ963514

RTI. (n.d.). *What is RTI?* Retrieved from http://www.rtinetwork.org/learn/what/whatisrti

Sciberras, E., Ohan, J., & Anderson, V. (2012). Bullying and peer victimization in adolescent girls with attention-deficit/v disorder. *Child Psychiatry of Human Development,* 43, 254-276. Retrieved from https://www.ncbi.nlm.nih.gov/pubmed/22038319

Swearer, J.M. & Hymel, S. (2015). Understanding the psychology of bullying: Moving toward a social-ecological diathesis-stress model. *American Psychologist,* 20(4), 344-353. Retrieved from https://www.ncbi.nlm.nih.gov/pubmed/25961315

Twyman, K.A. et al. (2010). Bullying and ostracism experiences in children with special health care needs. *Journal of Developmental and Behavioral Pediatrics*, 31(1), 1-8. Retrieved from https://www.ncbi.nlm.nih.gov/pubmed/20081430

Understood. (n.d.) The bullying problem: What you need to know. *Understood for Learning and Attention Issues*. Retrieved from https://www.understood.org/en/friends-feelings/common-challenges/bullying/the-bully- problem-what-you-need-to-know

United States Department of Education. (2017) *IDEA*. Retrieved from https://www.ed.gov/policy/speced/guid/idea/idea2004.html?exp=0

Willis, J. (2007). *Brain friendly strategies for the inclusion classroom*. Alexandria, VA: Association for Supervision and Curriculum Development.

Yang, S, Stewart, R., Kim, J.M., Shin, S., Dewey, M.E., Maskey, S, & Yoon, J.S. (2013). Differences in predictors of traditional and cyber-bullying: A 2-year longitudinal study in Korean school children. *European Child Adolescent Psychiatry*, 22, 309-318.

DOI:10.1007/s00787-012-0374-6 YouTube. (2013). *Megan Meier Story*. Retrieved from https://www.Youtube.com/watch?v=OIVU15R3xxA

Chapter 3

Learning Disabilities and Anxiety: Understanding and Addressing the Common Occurrence

Nicholas D. Young, *American International College*,
and Kristen L. Bonanno-Sotiropoulos,
Bay Path University

According to the US Department of Education (2014), approximately 4% of school-age children have a specific learning disability. Specific learning disabilities are the largest classification of students receiving services under special education at approximately 42% (National Center for Learning Disabilities, 2014). According to the Individuals with Disabilities Education Improvement Act of 2004, a specific learning disability "means a disorder in one or more of the basic psychological processes involved in understanding or in using language, spoken or written, that may manifest itself in the imperfect ability to listen, think, speak, read, write, spell, or to do mathematical calculations, including conditions such as perceptual disabilities, brain injuries, minimal brain function, dyslexia, and development aphasia" [34 CFR§300.8(c)(10)].

Research shows that children and adolescents with learning disabilities present with a variety of difficulties in academic, behavioral, social, and emotional domains (McGovern, Lowe, and Hill, 2016). Research has further established a clear connection between mental health problems and learning disabilities (Mammarella, Ghisi, Bomba, Bottesi, Caviola, Broggi, and Nacinovich, 2016; Milligan, Badali, & Spiroiu, 2015; Nelson & Harwood, 2011). Students with learning disabilities confront challenges with processing information, which puts them at a higher risk for experiencing emotional dysregulation (Mammarella, et. al., 2016).

Students with learning disabilities must rely on coping strategies in order to lessen or avoid the presence of challenging emotions, experiences, and tasks (Milligan, Badali, & Spiroiu, 2015). Within the behavioral domain, students with learning disabilities are twice as likely as students without learning disabilities to display externalizing behavioral problems within the clinical range. In addition, children and adolescents with learning disabilities tend to experience lower social standing with less social support than those peers without learning disabilities (McGovern, et al., 2016).

The Connection Between Learning Disabilities and Anxiety

Most educators understand and acknowledge that learning disabilities are commonly recognized for their impact on academic achievement; however, students with learning disabilities often experience difficulties that extend beyond the classroom walls (Tannock, 2013). Difficulties such as low academic self-confidence, low social competence, the feeling of rejection and neglect, symptoms of anxiety and depression, as well as unstable peer relationships (Milligan, et al., 2015). Anxiety and depression are the most common mental health problems among adolescents with learning disabilities, measuring at approximately 30% to 50% compared to only 10% to 20% of adolescents without learning disabilities (Ashraf & Najam, 2015).

Anxiety is a particular form of emotional distress frequently experienced by individuals with learning disabilities (Beauchemin, Hutchins, and Patterson, 2008; Nelson & Harwood, 2011). There are two minds of thought regarding the connection between learning disabilities and anxiety. Some researchers believe that anxiety develops as a result of learning difficulties, as academic achievement is central to childhood. Making adequate progress in reading, writing and mathematics is a major developmental task to be accomplished throughout the school years. Individuals who struggle to master academic skills may develop an anxiety reaction in anticipation of possible academic failure (Nelson& Harwood, 2011)

Other researchers believe that learning problems are caused by high levels of anxiety (Nelson& Harwood, 2011). In any case, higher levels of anxiety in children and adolescents with learning disabilities impede their academic progress by distracting them from learning or by leading them to avoid difficult schoolwork (McGovern, et al., 2016). Inquiry has indicated that high levels of anxiety have negative effects on cognitive performance on academic tasks.

Suffering from anxiety requires cognitive energy which, therefore, limits the storage component of the processing system (McGovern, et al., 2016; Nelson & Harwood, 2011). It is critical for educators to acknowledge that deficits in specific cognitive abilities such as working memory and metacognition are common characteristics of learning disabilities. Additional impairment in these cognitive processes resulting from anxiety may be debilitating for many individuals (McGovern, et. al., 2016; Swanson and Sachse-Lee, 2001).

Learning Disabilities and Anxiety in the Classroom

A 2011 study conducted by Nelson and Harwood revealed that approximately 70% of students with learning disabilities experience higher anxious symptomatology than their general education peers. This finding suggests that there should be concern that students with learning disabilities are at higher risk for potentially problematic anxiety-related distress within the school setting. As a result, schools need to explore ways to provide reasonable services that will be beneficial to decreasing anxiety within this population. Further, the authors stress that when anxiety symptoms are not addressed early they tend to become more severe and can lead to other forms of psychopathology such as depression (McGovern, et. al., 2016; Milligan, et. al., 2015; Nelson & Harwood, 2011).

Many have argued that the emotional needs of students with learning disabilities are often neglected because they were often served only for the academic side of their learning disability (Nelson & Harwood, 2011). Further understanding the level of anxiety commonly experienced by students with learning disabilities would assist educators in providing appropriate intervention services, thus, reducing anxiety symptoms and ultimately support academic gains (Tannock, 2013).

Nelson and Harwood (2011) suggest that teachers may not be adequately trained to address the emotional needs of students with learning disabilities. Therefore, teacher candidates in teacher preparation programs should be provided training not only in instructional strategies for students with learning disabilities but also strategies for coping with and reducing anxiety (Zenner, Hermleben-Kurz, & Walach, 2014).

Learning Disabilities and Depression

In addition to the substantiated connection between learning disabilities and anxiety, research has also linked the elevated occurrence of depression within this student population as well. Students with both reading disabilities and nonverbal learning disabilities tend to perform poorly at school and fail to achieve expected academic results as their typical peers. As a result, this becomes a risk factor for the onset of current and long-term psychological maladjustment. Studies have shown that difficulties at school may increase the risk of an individual suffering from internalizing disorders such as depression, anxiety, and social withdrawal (Mammarella, et al., 2016).

In a study conducted by Mammarella, et al. (2016), the occurrence of anxiety and depression were measured by students with nonverbal learning disabilities, reading disabilities, and students with typical development. Individuals with nonverbal learning disabilities as well as reading disabilities reported experiencing more generalized and social anxiety symptoms than students who were typically developing.

Students with non-verbal learning disabilities reported more severe anxiety pertaining to school as well as separation anxiety and depressive symptoms. Students with reading disabilities showed higher depressive symptoms than the other two groups combined. Similarly, Dahle, Knivsberg, and Andressen (2011), identified higher rates of depressive and withdrawal symptoms with students having reading disabilities compared to typically developing students.

Learning Disabilities, Anxiety, and Gender

Statistics indicate that the occurrence of anxiety and depressive symptoms are more prevalent in girls with learning disabilities than boys with learning disabilities (Ashraf & Najam, 2015; National Center for Learning Disabilities, 2014). On the other hand, boys with learning disabilities tend to display more externalizing behavior problems than internalizing symptoms.

A 2015 study conducted by Ashraf and Najam supported these statistics and revealed a significantly strong relationship between anxiety and depression among girls diagnosed as having a learning disability. In addition, this study also concluded that girls with learning disabilities who did not receive treatment for anxiety and/or depression symptoms were negatively impacted throughout life as evidenced by higher internalizing of behaviors including suicidal attempts (Ashraf & Najam, 2015).

Girls with learning disabilities present with more negative self-esteem, which is consistent with previous research (Ashraf & Najam, 2015). Specifically, adolescent girls with learning disabilities present with significantly high symptoms of phobic disorders, generalized anxiety, and significant depressive symptoms. The girls in the 2015 study showed 21% to 40% anxiety and depressive symptoms compared to only 14% of anxiety and depressive symptoms for girls without learning disabilities (Ashraf & Najam, 2015).

Strategies to Lessen the Effects of Anxiety in Students with Learning Disabilities

Social and Emotional Learning

One shift in education is the focus on preparing students with 21st-century skills. Cognitive, interpersonal, and interpersonal confidence are essential to building these skills (Pellegrino & Hilton, 2013). Social and emotional learning have been shown to influence positive academic performance even for students with disabilities (Durlak, Dymnicki, Taylor, Weissberg, and Schellinger, 2011). Knowing that social and emotional health directly impacts academic performance, 21st-century schools are investing in social and emotional learning opportunities to coincide with traditional academic areas (Gueldner & Feuerborn, 2016).

According to the Collaborative for Academic, Social and Emotional Learning (2014), social and emotional instruction promotes five person-centered interrelated components. These elements are essential to the cognitive, social, and emotional development of individuals. Person-centered areas of social-emotional learning include self-awareness, self-management, social-awareness, relationship-skills, and responsible decision-making.

Durlak, et al. (2011) conducted a meta-analysis focusing on universal school-wide social-emotional interventions and revealed significant improvements in both social and emotional skills, attitudes towards self and others, positive social behaviors, and increases in academic performance in both students with and without disabilities. In addition, there were decreases in conduct problems and emotional distress.

Mindfulness and Meditation

In addition to social-emotional learning strategies, there is an increased interest in the application of mindfulness practices within schools to promote wellness to both students as well as teachers (Meiklejohn, Phillips, Freedman, Griffin, Biegel, Roach, and Saltzman, 2012). Strategies embedded within mindfulness interventions include meditation, breathing techniques, and yoga. Mindfulness practices have been shown to remediate problem behaviors, mitigate risks, and promote well-being within youths displaying clinical mental health problems (Meiklejohn, et al., 2012).

Zenner, et. al. (2014), conducted a meta-analysis of twenty-four universal school-based mindfulness programs. Their analysis examined programs that focused on teaching relaxation and coping skills to all students regardless of their risk for experiencing social and emotional problems. The results of the studies indicated that mindfulness programs have the best outcomes on a student's ability to pay attention and ultimately make academic gains.

Milligan, et al. (2015) conducted a qualitative study of the effects of Integra Mindfulness Martial Arts (MMA) to address self-regulation challenges for students with learning disabilities. Integra Mindfulness Martial Arts (MMA) is an evidence-informed treatment that integrates mindfulness, cognitive therapy, and behavior modification into a martial arts training program.

This study consisted of adolescents between the ages of 8 and 10 labeled as having a learning disability comorbid with anxiety and/or behavioral concerns. These students participated in twenty weekly MMA sessions that lasted an hour and a half in length. Students were then interviewed with the results indicating that adolescents felt that learning about, and participating in, the mindfulness practices provided strategies that they could use to decrease patterns of emotional dysfunction and self-regulate their behaviors (Milligan, et al., 2015).

A 2008 study conducted by Beauchemin, Hutchins, and Patterson looked at the impact of a mindfulness and meditation intervention on anxiety levels of high school students diagnosed with learning disabilities. The study consisted of 10 minutes of meditation at the beginning of each class period, five days per week for five consecutive weeks. The results revealed significant decreases in anxiety symptoms and therefore minimizing cognitive interference which yielded positive academic outcomes across all participants Beauchemin, 2008; Gueldner & Feuerborn, 2016).

Gueldner and Feuerborn (2016) believe that programs teaching mindfulness-based practices can fall under the umbrella of social-emotional learning. Although mindfulness-based practices are unique in that they incorporate yoga, meditation, and breathing techniques, these practices offer similarities to components in social and emotional learning. Both mindfulness-based practices and social and emotional instruction occur within the school/classroom setting during a specific designated time, provide options for out of school/classroom practice, include the use of supportive materials such as videos and handouts, and can include parents and families in promoting practices at home.

Conclusion

The alarming number of students identified as having a learning disability, combined with the knowledge that these students are at a much higher risk for experiencing anxiety and depressive symptoms, calls for increased awareness and support within our classrooms (Nelson & Harwood, 2011). Students who present with combined deficits in academic performance and mental health symptoms are entering our classrooms at a disturbing rate (National Center for Learning Disabilities, 2014).

Strategies such as mindfulness and meditation, as well as social and emotional learning awareness are promising practices for decreasing the symptoms of anxiety and depression for students with learning disabilities (Gueldner & Feuerborn, 2016; Milligan, et. al., 2015; Zenner, et. al., 2014). Practicing mindfulness and meditation techniques within the classroom in simple ways introduce all students to tool and strategies that can be used to regulate behaviors (Meiklejohn, et. al., 2012). Both strategies focus on breathing techniques, visualization strategies, and simple yoga poses.

Social-emotional learning incorporates various areas that address the cognitive, social, and emotional development of all students (Collaborative for Academic, Social and Emotional Learning, 2014), In order to address the development of these areas, social and emotional instruction integrates instruction in self-awareness, self-management, social awareness, relationship-skills, and responsible decision-making skills. Instruction in these areas has been proven effective in supporting increased academic achievement (Pellegrino & Hilton, 2013).

Points to Remember

- *Approximately 42% of school-aged children receive special education services for a learning disability.*
- *Approximately 30% to 50% of students who are identified as having a learning disability experience symptoms of anxiety and depression.*

- *Girls with learning disabilities are more likely to experience negative self-esteem, depression and anxiety than boys with learning disabilities.*
- *If symptoms of anxiety and depression are not addressed early they tend to become more severe and can lead to other forms of psychopathology.*
- *Strategies such as social and emotional instruction, meditation, and mindfulness have been proven effective at decreasing the emotional symptomology experienced by many students with learning disabilities.*

References

Ashraf, f. and Najam, N. (2015). Comorbidity of anxiety disorder and major depression among girls with learning disabilities. *Pakistan Journal of Medical Research.* 54(4). Retrieved from https://www.researchgate.net/publication/304626930_Comorbidity_of_Anxiety_Disorder_and_Major_Depression_among_Girls_with_Learning_Disabilities

Beauchemin, J., Hutchins, T., and Patterson, F. (2008). Mindfulness meditation may lessen anxiety, promote social skills, and improve academic performance among adolescents with learning disabilities. *Complementary Health Practice Review.* 13(1). 35-45. DOI: 10.1177/1533210107311624

Dahle, A., Knivsberg, A., and Andressen, A. (2011). Coexisting problem behavior in severe dyslexia. *Journal of Research in Special Educational Needs.* 11. 162-170. Doi:10.1111/j.1471-3802.2010.01190

Durlak, J., Dymnicki, A., Taylor, R., Weissberg, R., and Schellinger, K. (2011). The impact of enhancing students' social and emotional learning: a meta-analysis of school based universal interventions. *Child Development.* 82. 405-432. doi/10.1111/j.1467-8624.2010.01564

Gueldner, B., and Feuerborn, L. (2016). Integrating mindfulness-based practices into social and emotional learning: a case application. *Mindfulness.* 7. 164-175. DOI: 10.1007/s12671-015-0423-6

Individuals with Disabilities Education Improvement Act. 34 CFR§612.8(c)(10), 2004.

Mammarella, I., Ghisi, M., Bomba, M., Bottesi, G., Caviola, S., Broggi, F., and Nacinovich, R. (2016). Anxiety and depression in children with nonverbal learning disabilities, reading disabilities, or typical development. *Journal of Learning Disabilities.* 49(2). 130-139. DOI:10.1177/0022219414529336

McGovern, J., Lowe, P., and Hill, J. (2016). Relationships between trait anxiety, demographic variables, and school adjustment in students with specific learning disabilities. *Journal of Child and Family Studies.* 25. 1724-1734. Retrieved from https://link.springer.com/article/10.1007/s10826-015-0348-7

Meiklejohn, J., Phillips, C., Freedman, M., Griffin, M., Biegel, G., Roach, A., and Saltzman, A. (2012). Integrating mindfulness training into K12 education: fostering the resilience of teachers and students. *Mindfulness.* 3(4). 291-307. DOI: 10.1007/s12671-012-0094-5

Milligan, K., Badali, P., and Spiroiu, F. (2015). Using integra mindfulness martial arts to address self-regulation challenges in youth with learning disabilities: a qualitative exploration. *Journal of Child and Family Studies.* 24. 562-575. DOI:10.1007/s10826-013-9868-1

National Center for Learning Disabilities (2014). *The state of learning disabilities* (3rd ed.). Retrieved from http://www.ncld.org/wp-content/uploads/2014/11/2014-State-of-LD.pdf

Nelson, J., and Harwood, H. (2011). Learning disabilities and anxiety: A meta-analysis. *Journal of Learning Disabilities.* 44(1). 3-17. DOI:10.1177/0022219409359939

Pellegrino, J., and Hilton, M. (Eds.) (2013). *Education for life and work: developing transferable knowledge and skills in the 21st century.* Washington, DC: National Academies Press.

Swanson, H. and Sachse-Lee, C. (2001). A subgroup of analysis of working memory in children with reading disabilities: Domain-general or domain-specific deficiency? *Journal of Learning Disabilities.* 34. 249-263. DOI:10.1177/002221940103400305

Tannock, R. (2013). Rethinking ADHD and LD in DSM-5: proposed changes in diagnostic criteria. *Journal of Learning Disabilities.* 46(1). 5-25. DOI:10.1177/0022219412464341

U.S. Department of Education. Office of Special Education and Rehabilitative Services. Office of Special Education Programs. (2014). *36th annual report to congress on the implementation of the individuals with disabilities education act, 2014 (vol. 1).* Retrieved from https://www2.ed.gov/about/reports/annual/osep/2014/parts-b-c/36th-idea-arc.pdf

Zenner, C., Hermleben-Kurz, S., and Walach, H. (2014). Mindfulness based interventions in Schools: A systematic review and meta-analysis. *Frontiers in Psychology,* 5. Retrieved from: https://www.ncbi.nlm.nih.gov/pubmed/25071620

Chapter 4

Reading, Writing, and Rap: Using Rhyme to Inspire Emotional and Academic Growth

Rosalie Fink, *Lesley University*

A growing body of research suggests that optimal emotional and academic growth and engagement occur when teachers and therapists integrate students' interests and their favorite musical genres into therapy and academic lessons (Fink, 2017, 2015; Murray, 2015; Renninger & Hidi, 2016; Rinne et al, 2011). By enlisting students' out-of-school interests (such as rap), teachers and therapists can facilitate experiences for students with LD that are more meaningful and memorable - academically, socially, and emotionally (Fink, 2017, 2015; Renninger & Hidi, 2016).

Based on his theory of multiple intelligences, Howard Gardner has emphasized the importance of utilizing the arts and multisensory approaches to education (Gardner, 1999). At The Excellence in Special Education Summit, Gardner urged educators "to teach important concepts and ideas pluralistically" (Gardner, 2014). By this, Gardner explained, he meant teaching with rhythm, rhyme, and other multisensory modalities through the arts (Gardner, 2014). Gardner's reason was clear and straightforward: If you teach pluralistically, using all of the senses and the arts whenever possible, then you reach more students, including students with learning disabilities.

The Importance of Rap and Poetry

Long before the rap musical "Hamilton" became a hit Broadway success, teachers and therapists intuitively knew that rhythm and rhyme have the power to embed information deep in memory. Everyone recalls songs, nursery rhymes, prayers, and poems that were learned as early as ages 4, 5, or 6---before learning to read. The reason it is easy to remember detailed information from these early learning experiences is that rhythm and rhyme have a magnetic ability to embed words and concepts deep in our brains.

Rap and Classic Poetry

Increasingly, teachers today are using the power of rhythm and rhyme to engage students in deep learning through the use of rap and poetry (Fink, 2015, 2017; Hong Xu, 2008; Sitomer & Cirrelli, 2004; Koch & Farrell, 1982). In a compelling book, *Hip-Hop Poetry and the Classics*, Sitomer & Cirelli (2004) argue convincingly that rap lyrics possess the same literary components as classical poems by Keats and Shelly. They show that both rap and poetry can be used effectively for teaching. The authors demonstrate that rap and poetry both include multiple elements in common: alliteration, allusion, figurative language, hyperbole, imagery, irony, theme, metaphor, simile, mood creation, onomatopoeia, personification, symbolism, rhythmic patterns, and rhyme schemes.

Spurred by Sitomer & Cirelli's (2004) compelling arguments as well as Hong Xu's research on the effectiveness of popular culture texts (Hong Xu, 2008, 2007), a study was conducted to explore rap and poetry as teaching tools in English composition and special education literacy classes took place. The purpose was to harness the enormous appeal of rap and poetry in order to enliven lessons and reach all types of students, especially students with LD.

The Teacher-Researcher Methodology

A teacher study based on Cochran-Smith & Lytle's method of practitioner research was conducted that involved systematic observation, notation, and data analysis by the teacher-researcher (Cochran-Smith & Lytle, 2009). In this study, rap and poetry were used as teaching strategies in my undergraduate English composition classes and my master's degree level special education literacy classes. The study took place at a mid-sized university in the Northeastern region of the USA. Classes were inclusive and consisted of 20-25 students each. During the five years of the study, the total number of participants was approximately 500 students; about 125 of them had documented learning disabilities (LD). Students with LD had previously disclosed their learning differences and submitted documentation to The Office of Learning Disabilities. In addition, students with LD presented summaries of their specific needs for reasonable accommodations to the researcher.

Many of the students were the first in their families to attend college. Often, they came steeped in deep knowledge of popular culture and admiration for popular art forms. Given my students' backgrounds and their abiding interests in popular culture, the researcher set out to explore novel ways to capitalize on their familiarity with rap and use it in the classroom.

Observing Rap in The Classroom

Based on observations, notation records, and analyses, rap was found to be a constructive way to promote students' positive mental health development and, simultaneously, help them develop strong literacy skills. Guiding students to write their own raps about various emotions and challenging social experiences proved to be especially successful. Creating their own raps inspired students' enthusiasm and enhanced their ability to analyze their own emotions as well as those of others. Creative rap writing also helped my students learn to read complex texts closely, review text content in great detail, and relate challenging, higher-level texts in meaningful ways to their own lives. When students invented a new rap themselves, they experienced the excitement and joy of creation and a genuine sense of accomplishment and pride. Their success bolstered their self-confidence.

Implementing Rap with The Rap Protocol

After students had read an assigned chapter (or book) and had discussed the text in small groups or as a whole class the rap was implemented. The teacher explained that rap could help them review and deepen this understanding of what they had read. To guide students in the rap-writing process, a set of sequential steps of The Rap Protocol was created. The Rap Protocol guides students to create their own original raps with the purpose of developing strong reading, writing, presentation, and social-emotional skills. By using this step-by-step protocol, the researcher was able to implement rap successfully as a creative tool for teaching. Since rap is written in iambic pentameter, rap music typically conveys the feeling of being behind the beat. Many students today know the rhythms of rap based on their own experiences listening to popular music. Students' familiarity with rap, as well as the sequential structure of The Rap Protocol, helped them compose raps of their own. The Rap Protocol consists of six steps:

- First, tell students or clients to use rhythm and rhyme to write a rap about their chapter, book, or experience. Explain that not every line must rhyme. (In addition, encourage the use of alliteration and rhymes within a line.)

- Explain that raps should use language appropriate for performing publicly in school.

- After students write a rap, have them practice reading it aloud expressively and rhythmically---adding gestures, clapping, body movement, or costumes if they wish.

- Next, guide students to perform their raps for the class. An additional option is to record their performances; then post them on a classroom website or blog. (Students can also perform their raps live for families, school assemblies, nursing homes, and so forth.)

- Display students' raps on bulletin boards or school display cases. In addition, help students publish their work in school newsletters or online student newspapers.

- Encourage students and clients to create artwork that illustrates a feeling or idea from the rap; then display the artwork.

Adapting the Rap Protocol

The Rap Protocol can be easily adapted for many types of therapy sessions, school subjects, ages, and grade levels. It is a flexible tool that can be used in individual therapy sessions, whole group sessions, pairs or dyads, or small groups. In conducting this study, the researcher noticed that The Rap Protocol worked especially well when therapists and teachers used a gradual release of responsibility approach. This meant that teachers and therapists slowly and gradually relinquished responsibility from themselves to their students or clients. As students and clients worked in pairs or small groups, they learn the step-by-step sequence of The Rap Protocol and became increasingly adept and independent as rap artists.

The researcher observed that the more experiences students were given to create original raps, the more independent they became in using rap as an art form and learning tool. Creating new raps to encapsulate emotions and summarize ideas was especially useful for helping students with LD understand feelings and synthesize information about emotions---their own as well as those of characters in books. While students were busy creating their raps, the researcher circulated around the room and observed them intensely engaged in deep discussions about a variety of emotions, behaviors, vocabulary, and concepts.

The researcher noticed that all kinds of raps worked well for helping students with LD master both academic and social/emotional skills---published raps, teacher/therapist-created raps, and student-created raps. Results showed that student-created raps were an especially effective way for students with LD to consolidate what they had learned from reading about a topic, including topics about positive ways to deal with mental health issues.

The success of these early experiments allowed the researcher to become increasingly more comfortable with integrating rap into my English composition and special education literacy lessons. Rap was used effectively on a regular basis to help students with LD review for weekly quizzes, midterms, and other tests and assessments. As the researcher developed familiarity with teaching rap, it was introduced at hands-on workshops, lectures and various education conferences where teachers, special educators, therapists, and coaches created their own raps about emotions.

Using Rap to Identify Emotions

Many students with LD lack understanding of their own feelings and the feelings of others. Their inadequate social-emotional understanding leaves them vulnerable and unprepared to respond appropriately in complex social situations. Consequently, they can benefit from explicit lessons and activities on naming specific emotions.

"Name That Feeling" is a rap that was written by therapists and special educators at a hands-on workshop given at The Asperger/Autism Network (AANE) in Waltham, Massachusetts. The purpose of this rap is to help individuals with LD become aware of their own feelings through the direct labeling of emotions. "Name That Feeling" can be used by therapists and teachers as a springboard for fruitful discussions about various emotions: how to recognize them, how to respond appropriately to them, and so forth.

Name That Feeling

by Maggie Thomson, Sandra Watson, Cathy Lunetta, and Melody Skall

Name that feeling,

Don't send yourself reeling.

Figure it out; don't pout!

Bring it up from inside,

Don't let that feeling hide.

Happy, mad, sometimes sad,

Frustrated, agitated, sometimes glad.

Explain to people how you feel.

Don't hold back; just be real!

After reading, discussing, and chanting "Name That Feeling", teachers and therapists can provide explicit instruction and lead discussions and role-plays about appropriate behavioral responses to challenging emotional and social situations. Students with LD are likely to benefit greatly from these types of rap-infused activities focused on emotions.

Using Rap for Test-taking

Test-taking creates both academic and emotional challenges for all types of students, especially those with LD. Yet, today's students are required to take numerous tests in order to meet state and national standards. Teachers and therapists must prepare students with LD for the academic and emotional challenges of taking tests. One way is to provide direct instruction in good test-taking techniques. To prepare her students academically and emotionally for the rigors of Massachusetts state tests, for example, a third-grade educator in an inner-city school in Boston, Massachusetts provided direct instruction in several excellent test-taking strategies. After discussing each strategy in detail, she used The Rap Protocol to engage students in reviewing good test-taking strategies as they prepared for the Massachusetts Comprehensive Assessment System (MCAS) test. Each student created one line of "The MCAS Rap". Students took ownership by stating their names, each student adding another important test-taking strategy. Here is the rap that they co-created:

The MCAS Rap

Chorus

We are here today

To rap about a test

Called The MCAS

So you can do your best.

Verse 1

My name is Kenisha and the first thing that you do

Is to read the directions all the way through.

My name is TJ and the next step that you take

Is to read the title; don't take a break.

My name is Savari, and the next thing that you do

Is to read the italics; that is what you do.

My name is Erin, and the fourth thing that you do

Is to read the questions, then go back and review.

Chorus

Verse 2

My name is Bill, and after we review,

You start the story; that is what you do.

My name is Chris, and when we find the answer

We make sure to highlight to get the right answer.

My name is Deidre, and I have a suggestion:

After you highlight, read the next question.

My name is Maya, and we've shown you the way

To conquer the MCAS, so have a nice day!

Collaboratively creating and chanting The MCAS Rap helped these third-graders improve their test-taking skills and increase their self-confidence, thus promoting positive mental health and enhancing their overall emotional well-being.

Using Rap to Make Smooth Transitions

Students with LD frequently have trouble making transitions and may become emotionally overwhelmed transitioning from one activity to another. Giving students prior notice a few minutes in advance helps them get mentally and psychologically ready for a change of activities. Moreover, using a transitional rap, such as "The Clean Up Time Rap", can help them make transitions more smoothly. "The Clean Up Time Rap" is fun and provides an excellent way to help young students in grades pre-K-2 make transitions and learn classroom routines. This rap was composed by a teacher and is meant as a "call and response" rap. First, the teacher says, "Ring-a-ding-ding! Hear the chime?" Then students respond, "Clean-up time! Clean-up time!" Next, the teacher asks, "Dirty floor?" and students answer, "Not anymore," and so on.

Clean-up Time Rap

by Dona Rice

Ring-a-ding-ding!

(Teacher uses a bell, tambourine, or drum)

Hear the chime?

Clean-up time!

Clean-up time!

Dirty floor?

Not anymore!

Messy desks?

We won't rest!

Books off rack?

Put them back!

Toys askew?

That won't do!

Come on team!

Let's get clean!

Using Rap to Respond to Books

Student-created raps are excellent for responding to books and develop deep understanding of complex texts. In this study, writing their own raps was particularly useful for helping students with learning disabilities understand complex emotions and family relationships. In addition, composing their own raps also gave these students an effective way to review what they had read and prepare to write persuasive essays about complex books. Many students also created lively gestures and body movements to accompany the words and accentuate the rhythms of their raps. Here are a few examples of student-created raps in response to books they read in English composition.

The first rap, "Daddy Wasn't There", was written by students after they read Barack Obama's *Dreams from My Father: A Story of Race and Inheritance.* This rap recreates the moment in President Obama's life when, at age 21, he received a phone call from his aunt in Nairobi, Africa. She informed him of the death of his biological father, who had left the family when Obama was 3 years old. After deserting his wife and young son, Obama's father had visited only once, when Obama was 10. Nevertheless, Obama continued to yearn for his father and always dreamt of someday being reunited with him. The following student-created rap movingly expresses Obama's eternal yearning for his absentee dad--a situation faced by many students today.

Daddy Wasn't There

by Hannah Brosnan and Rose Heller

Sitting in the kitchen

Cooking up some breakfast

Got a phone call

And my life was re-directed.

My aunt from Nairobi

Was like "Listen up Barry"

Your dad passed away

I am so sorry."

STOP! REWIND!

I don't know what to feel

I don't know what to think.

The death of a father

Flashed by in a blink.

Tension in the air,

Daddy wasn't there.

Tension in the air,

Daddy wasn't there.

Memories I knew only from stories

Cried myself to sleep over all of these worries,

Daddy where'd you go? Daddy where ya been?

Never thought we'd meet again, said goodbye when I was ten.

Dreams from my father

Yearning is a bother

Daddy wasn't there

Guess I shouldn't care...

...BUT I DO!

Absentee fathers, good parents, parental substitutes, and other important topics are embedded throughout President Obama's moving memoir, *Dreams From My Father*. As students read this complex text, they engaged in thoughtful, animated discussions about the parenting traits of each adult in young Obama's life. They composed in-class free-writes--- short, quickly written paragraphs about the characteristics of their ideal parent. After sharing their free-writes (with the whole class or with a partner), students followed The Rap Protocol, which helped them compose original raps about the salient qualities of a good parent. "A Good Parent Loves Unconditionally" is a student-created rap written in response to Obama's memoir.

A Good Parent Loves Unconditionally

by Todd R. Neill

A good parent loves unconditionally,

Reading, Writing, and Rap   53

Is always there physically and emotionally,

Is patient and calm in face of calamity.

A good parent teaches

Honesty and modesty,

And keeps lofty goals within reach.

Instilling values in each child,

While always being calm and mild.

A good parent loves unconditionally.

In addition to reading Obama's memoir, my English composition students also read and wrote raps in response to Karin Cook's coming-of-age tale, *What Girls Learn*. This engaging novel deals with the relationship between two sisters, ages 11 and 12. Consequently, sibling rivalry is the theme of the next rap written by students in response to this interesting, fast-paced book, which was later made into a movie.

Sibling Rivalry

by Molly Wyman and Michelle Goldberg

We fight about clothes

'Cause you steal my sweaters,

And sometimes we argue

But it's all for the better.

We look out for each other

From dating to looks,

And when you need help

I crack open the books.

Our fights don't last long

Even though they're intense,

We can't stay mad long

'Cause our love is immense!

As students discussed *What Girls Learn,* several open-ended, thought-provoking questions were posed to guide reflection and discussion: Why do people lie? Under what circumstances, if any, is it okay to lie? What long-term negative effects may ensue? How do you feel when you tell a lie? In the novel, *What Girls Learn*, these important questions are considered in the context of a family's responses to a mother's diagnosis of breast cancer. "Euphemisms, Dark Secrets, White Lies Too" is a student-created rap that addresses the complex issue of secrecy and lies explored in this intriguing novel.

Euphemisms, Dark Secrets, White Lies Too

by Todd R. Neill

In school one day Tilden gets an invitation

To see a movie about menstruation.

She hides the invite 'til the right time to tell

'Cause right about now Mama isn't doing well.

Her doctor's appointment isn't routine;

She'll be in the hospital a week, it seems.

They learn that Mama has a lump in her breast,

It could be cancer, they'll find out from the test.

Tilden and her sister and Nick are on edge,

They go to visit Mama and stand near her bed.

Tilden gets mad and feels really, really sick

When she learns that Mama told her secret just to Nick.

Euphemisms, dark secrets, white lies too,

Do they ever really help, or just hurt you?

Euphemisms, dark secrets, white lies too,

Do they ever really help, or just hurt you?

While students wrote raps about *What Girls Learn*, the researcher circulated around the room and observed students actively discussing issues of privacy, secrecy, life, and death---issues with deep emotional and moral significance that impact all of our lives. These challenging issues may be especially daunting for students with LD. The researcher observed students engaged in thoughtful serious discussions as showed the seriousness with which they reflected on what they had read. Their intense attention, enthusiastic participation, and consistent engagement were palpable. Creating raps about *What Girls Learn* helped students deepen their text understanding, review for tests, and prepare to write coherent essays with logical arguments about the novel's themes.

To help students develop skills in persuasive argument writing, they were given explicit instruction in the key components of an effective argument: a clearly expressed claim, a counterargument, detailed supporting evidence, and a clearly articulated conclusion. Then, to help the students review what had been learned, the teachers taught them "The Argument Rap". Researcher created, this rap helped students enumerate and review each aspect of a solidly written argument.

The Argument Rap

Let's analyze an argument

What must it contain?

The first component

Is the argument's claim.

Some call the claim "the thesis"

It's the author's main idea.

The important thing about it?

It's a statement, and it's clear.

Where should you put the claim?

Beginning? Middle? End?

Any place can work

But there's usually a trend.

Often the first paragraph

States the claim there.

But sometimes the claim

Appears elsewhere.

The second component

Is called the evidence:

Data, details, facts, and reasons

Used to convince.

To convince your readers

That your argument is tight,

Use facts and examples

To convince them of its might.

Explain each fact fully

So they know you're right.

Reasoning and logic

Make your argument tight.

Raise rebuttals or counterarguments

To show your awareness and strengthen your position.

Concede any weakness in your argument,

Acknowledge the strengths of the opposition.

Finally, your argument needs to end

With a clear conclusion, to avoid confusion.

To give your argument an awesome end,

Write a clear conclusion. Write a clear conclusion.

Restate your claim

And if you want to be creative,

End with a new question;

That's sure to get attention!

As students recited this rap, their faces were animated. Clearly, the students seemed to enjoy reciting "The Argument Rap". This was an engaging way for them remember each essential component of a persuasive essay.

Clap, Snap, and Move!

In addition to reciting "The Argument Rap", adding gesture and movement increased student engagement. Gesture and movement can be added to any rap to add rhythmic emphasis and fun. For example, once students are familiar with the words of "The Argument Rap" (or any other rap), the teacher can model and encourage them to recite it while they simultaneously clap hands, snap fingers, or bend knees up and down to the rhythm. Encourage students to choreograph simple body movements and steps they can perform while chanting the rap. In addition, the teacher can guide students to do a simple "One, Two, Three, Kick" side step, by following these steps:

- Move sideways to the left in 4/4 beat: Step on left foot, step on right foot, step on left foot, kick right foot raised slightly in the air to the front and across body to the left.

- Move sideways to the right in 4/4 beat. Step on right foot, step on left foot, step on right foot, kick left foot raised slightly in the air and across the body to the right.

- Repeat #1 and #2 until the end of the rap.

After the students had learned "The Argument Rap" and completed writing their essays, their papers were analyzed and found to be clear, coherent, and well-developed: overall, their papers contained each component of a strong logical argument. Apparently, learning, chanting, and moving to the rhythm of "The Argument Rap" had helped them master the components of this important genre of writing.

Reading and Writing Poetry

According to Kenneth Koch and Kate Farrell, reading and writing poetry are natural, worthwhile activities for all students, including those with learning disabilities (Koch & Farrell, 1982). Moreover, Koch & Farrell (1982) point out that students with LD and students with psychological and social problems are often very good at writing poetry, because writing poetry often "...gives students with LD confidence, which they haven't succeeded in getting from other parts of their education" (Koch & Farrell, 1982, p. 301).

Koch & Farrell (1982) also highlight the key role that emotions play not only in writing poems, but also in reading them. They suggest that a good way to help students enter the realm of poetry fearlessly and enthusiastically is for the teacher first to read many poems aloud. Then, encourage students to choose any poem that they like, selecting what appeals to them on an emotional level. According to Koch & Farrell (1982), who taught poetry in K-12 schools in New York City for many years, it's best not to analyze the meaning of a poem too soon; rather, encourage students to start by choosing a poem that they like and focus on what appeals to them about the poem: a feeling, a tone, an attitude, a topic, and so forth. Once students have chosen a poem that they like, they can use that poem as a model for composing their own poem.

Composing Poems Based on Models

Writing poetry using famous poems as models is an excellent way to promote positive mental health in students with LD and, simultaneously, promote academic success. This approach can be used successfully to help students with LD explore what they like about poems, enable them to delve deeply into emotional topics and feelings, and help them develop self-confidence and pride in their own writing ability. Composing-By-Model is effective for teaching typically developing students as well as students with a wide variety of learning challenges ----from mild learning disabilities to severe autism (Koch & Farrell, 1982).

To use the Composing-By-Model approach, the teacher introduces students to poems by famous poets, reading poems several times aloud. Maya Angelou and Walt Whitman are two examples of favorite poets with whom many students relate. After students listen to poems read aloud, the teacher guides them to create their own original poems about feelings and behavior, using the rhythm and structure of a famous poem as a model. The model poem provides a roadmap to guide students while they compose. Koch and Farrell's celebrated book, *Sleeping on the Wing: An Anthology of Modern Poetry with Essays on Reading and Writing*, contains rich selections of vibrant poems with instructional suggestions for teachers to use in their classrooms (Koch & Farrell, 1982).

Many teachers have used the Compose-By-Model strategy successfully with their own students in K-12 schools and clinics. Composing with a model is applicable for students of all ages, developmental stages, and ability levels. Two examples illustrate the success of this interesting approach to reading and writing poetry. Ben Feldman, a 7th grader, composed a moving poem, "Imprisoned Boy", based on "Caged Bird" by Nobel laureate Maya Angelou. Ben was told to write a poem on a topic of personal interest, using the format and structure of a poem that he liked. He chose Maya Angelou's poem "Caged Bird" as a model and followed the basic structure of Maya Angelou's poem. After completing his unique poem, "Imprisoned Boy", Ben was so proud of his accomplishment that he wrote, "P.S. I made it on my own!" Ben's note reveals his own pride of achievement; his moving poem of a boy in prison unearths feelings of deep emotional fear and hurt. Similar emotions are often experienced by children with LD, who are frequently bullied and ostracized. Here is Ben's poem.

Imprisoned Boy by Ben Feldman

The carefree boy

Runs through the forest,

The scent of pine

All around,

Eating candy,

Pound after pound.

But a boy who

Walks in his cell

Can almost smell

The scent of freedom.

His hands are cuffed

And his every move

Is being watched,

So he cries for his family,

Cries for his family.

The imprisoned boy cries,

Scared of his narrow path,

For the things he needs to have.

He cries so long

That the guards come along

And deprive him of his pride.

The carefree boy horses around

And wanders through the forest,

Finds a dollar bill,

Lying on the hill,

And then he pays

For a horseback ride.

But the imprisoned boy

Stands on the brink of despair

So sad he can barely breathe the air.

His hands are cuffed

And his every move is being watched.

So he cries for his family,

Cries for his family.

The imprisoned boy cries,

Scared of his narrow path,

For the things he needs to have.

He cries so long

That the guards come along

And deprive him of his pride.

They deprive him of his pride.

In Ben's poem, the imprisoned boy repeatedly "cries for his family". For many students with LD, families provide essential emotional comfort and the only respite they get from daily torments at school. Ben's creative poem conveys intense feelings and experiences. His teacher's guidance and encouragement enabled Ben to express deep feelings poetically. These experiences reading and writing poetry were invaluable to Ben's academic growth and mental health development. Ben's original poem provided a positive venue for him to demonstrate what he had learned academically about poetry. And, it was also a positive venue for him to express his emotions as a boy with learning disabilities. By expressing emotions through this beautifully written poem and receiving praise for his creative writing, Ben developed confidence in his writing ability and a stronger sense of himself as a competent, intelligent person.

The next poem was written by 10-year-old Nadia, who has autism and is minimally verbal. Nadia chose Walt Whitman's famous "Song of Myself" as her model. Nadia's poem, "Song of Myself: A Pebble", expresses how she feels as a person with autism: isolated, misunderstood, unable to make her thoughts and feelings known to the world. This moving poem reveals Nadia's heartfelt yearning to have her intelligence and feelings recognized.

Song of Myself: A Pebble

By Nadia Sohn Fink

I sing a song of all pebbles,

Each little stone baffling us people.

Pebbles are not meant to know pleasures like song.

Can you be a pebble and not sing?

I know life as a pebble.

Pebbles sing and know (as) voices united as one.

All, even pebbles, are part of the song.

Nadia's metaphor of herself as a pebble is a powerful expression of her thoughts and emotions, frustrations and desires to be heard. Significantly, this vibrant, emotional poem has literally given voice to this girl who is minimally verbal. Nadia's teachers skillfully used Koch and Farrell's method, using model poems to spur Nadia's creativity. They effectively combined this approach to poetry with The Rapid Prompting Method (RPM) for teaching students with autism expressive and receptive language. With RPM the student picks from two-word choices, then proceeds to pointing and spelling on an alphabet chart--- first in single words, then phrases, then sentences, and beyond (Mukhopadhyay, 2017, 2008).

By combining RPM with the Compose-By-Model approach, Nadia's teachers succeeded in enabling her to read and write poetry and take pride in her accomplishments. This opportunity to write poetry was a turning point for Nadia and led to a period of remarkable growth for her, both academically and emotionally. When asked if she wanted her poem to be published, Nadia didn't hesitate for a moment. Exuberantly, she typed, "Yes" on her computer keyboard.

Nadia was not only able to write expressive poetry, but perhaps most significantly, she was proud of her own achievement. This was both an academic milestone and a positive mental health moment for Nadia.

Conclusion

Nadia and Ben are fortunate to have teachers and therapists skilled in strategies that simultaneously promote academic growth and positive mental health development. To reach - and successfully teach - all kinds of students requires teachers who are knowledgeable and courageous and willing to try innovative approaches that spur growth and development in their students. The integration of rap and poetry into the curriculum is both exciting and important. These types of innovations can enable teachers to capture the attention and engage all types of students in meaningful learning, including students with LD; nothing is more important than that.

Points to Remember

- *Integrating rap and poetry into academic lessons and therapeutic sessions improves engagement, promotes deep learning, enhances memory and content retention, and promotes positive mental health for all types of students, including students with learning disabilities (LD).*

- *Student-created raps are especially useful for promoting self-confidence, deep understanding, the ability to synthesize complex information, and positive mental health for all types of students, especially students with LD*

- *The Rap Song Protocol is a step-by-step procedure that successfully guides students with LD to create their own unique raps. It is easy to follow and implement and has been used successfully with students across ages, grades, and ability levels.*

- *The Compose-With-A-Model Strategy for writing poetry improves academic growth and mental health development for students with a wide range of learning disabilities.*

- *Integrating rap and poetry into the curriculum enables teachers and therapists to capture the attention and spur meaningful learning in all students, including students with learning disabilities.*

References

Cochran-Smith, M. & Lytle, S. (2009). *Inquiry as stance: Practitioner research for the next generation.* New York, NY: Teachers College Press.

Fink, R. (2017). Rap and technology teach the art of argument. *Learning Disabilities: A Contemporary Journal*, 15(1), 39-53. Retrieved from https://eric.ed.gov/?id=EJ1141983

Fink, R. (2015). *Reading, writing, and rhythm: Engaging content-area literacy strategies.* Huntington Beach, CA: Shell Education.

Gardner, H. (2014). *Multiple Intelligences (MI) theory: Implications for teaching and learning.* The Whitehead Institute for Biomedical Research, Massachusetts Institute of Technology, Cambridge, MA, April 2, 2014.

Gardner, H. (1999). *Intelligence reframed: Multiple intelligences for the 21st century.* New York, NY: Basic Books.

Hong Xu, S. (2008). *Using popular culture texts to engage students in meaningful literacy learning.* Paper presented at the 19th Annual Summer Literacy Institute, Adelphi University, Garden City, New York, August 12, 2008.

Hong Xu, S., Zunich, L.O., & Perkins, R.S. (2007). *Trading cards to comic strips: Popular culture texts and literacy learning in grades K-8.* Newark, DE: The International Reading Association.

Koch, K. & Farrell (2016/1982). *Sleeping on the wing: An anthology of modern poetry with essays on reading and writing.* New York: Random House.

Mukhopadhyay, S. (2017). *Developing the Visual Skill of Reading Using Rapid Prompting Method.* July 12, 2017-Kindle edition.

Mukhopadhyay, S. (2008). *Understanding Autism Through Rapid Prompting Method.* Denver, CO: Outskirts Press.

Murray, M. (2015). *Behavioral relevance of single-trial learning from multisensory processes. Multisensory development, plasticity, and learning: From basic to clinical science.* Paper presented at the Symposium of The Annual Meeting of The American Association for the Advancement of Science, San Jose, CA.

Renninger, K. A. & Hidi, S. E. (2016). *The power of interest for motivation and engagement.* New York, NY: Routledge.

Rinne, L., Gregory, E., Yarmolinskayay, J., & Hardiman, M. (2011). Why arts integration improves long-term retention of content. *Mind, Brain, and Education*, 5(2), 89-96.doi/10.1111/j.1751-228X.2011.01114

Sitomer, A.L. & Cirelli, M. (2004). *Hip-hop poetry and the classics.* Beverly Hills, CA: Milk Mug Press.

Chapter 5

The Comforting Presence of Visual Literacy Skill in the English Language Arts Classroom

James D. Shivers, *University of Connecticut, The Yale Center for British Art*

English Language Arts curriculum often excludes multimodal discourse. Teachers, then, have limited options in working with students who have difficulties with the formal requirements for an ELA curriculum. Use of multimodal discourse is viewed as a non-academic, non-critical move where students are getting a reduced curriculum. Multimodal discourse is rarely viewed as an asset to critical growth, or as an asset to mental and cognitive health. Sometimes, teachers in ELA programs create 'creative projects' at the end of a unit, but don't explore how the process itself, as a practice, could offer avenues for creating emotional, creative, and critical growth throughout the entire year for all students. Instead visual literacy, and even media literacy, is viewed as something secondary, or only for students in lower level courses, or for those students who have difficulties with reading, writing, or speaking.

Contrary to the dominant mode of English Language Arts (ELA) delivery, visual experience and multimodal experience are valid forms of knowing, communicating, and building social connections with the world. Students arrive in our classrooms with incredible visual strengths that are often ignored or neglected. The visual strengths can be used to address all kinds of learners, all kinds of readers, all kinds of writers. Practicing visual literacy builds attention, stamina, and more awareness of the self, the world, and others. The ability to calmly monitor one's thoughts, actions, and learning is a life skill and promotes wellness. The practice of this skill set in the ELA classroom fosters language growth and a growing confidence in reading and writing.

The practices and stances to follow were designed for a regular education inclusive classroom, grades 9-12. On average, each class and level of course had twenty to thirty with disabilities or students at risk. In some classes the ratio was much higher. The goal of classroom practice was to create assignments that embraced multimodal discourse, encouraged the students as persons, employed their visual strengths, and fostered language growth in some capacity. Over the years, these practices, stances, course and assignment designs have had an enormous impact on student self-confidence, language growth, creativity and critical awareness. No one lesson fits all, but lessons that invite all make the classroom a healthier place for students who struggle with the ELA curriculum.

Context

The world has changed and the experience of children walking into the classroom is completely different than the previous generation's experience growing up. This is true for teachers as well as parents. Children are working out how to see and know in a completely different environment than before. Multimodal discourse dominates the student purview; thus, it is important to use visual strengths to foster critical and creative language and life growth. Including multimodal discourse in the ELA curriculum provides multiple ways to address all learners within an inclusive classroom.

Before laying a practical groundwork for such a practice, it is important to address some assumptions about the ELA classroom. Many outside the classroom assume that in a 'normal' classroom all students are similar readers and writers. Furthermore, inclusive classrooms have a range of learning disabilities at play: physical, emotional, cognitive (Shivers, Levenson, & Tan, 2017). Many inside the discipline assume that all language rules are established and fixed throughout time: grammar, syntax, spelling. Further, many assume that writing is a fixed process with only a few types of writing: expository, narrative, argumentative, persuasive (Lindemann, 2001). These writing forms are often taught in the secondary education context by teachers who are not required to publish regularly. Often it is assumed that only struggling readers and writers need visual aids and the use of multimodal discourse. And finally, many teachers do not regularly complete the assignments they assign.

Before educators speak or begin working with students, they must consider the basic goal: to increase language fluency: speaking, writing, reading. Given the form of tests and the demands of college expectations, it is a serious task to make sure students can (1) read and write effectively; (2) read in-between the lines; and (3) write outside the clichéd box. Educators must do this in a group setting, within a larger system of demands.

If educators pay attention to the lived experience of students it is clear their dominant experience of language is multimodal (Rushkoff & Dretzin, 2010; Rideout, Foeh, & Roberts, 2010). In other words, communication now fuses together letters, but also sounds, images, frames with still and moving images, and this is different than the material in the ELA classroom.

Thinking of this visually, students must, without fail, follow the ruler to the end of the page, then return. If they look away, if their eye scans, if they don't endure, waiting, to see, while holding the line, they will not 'follow' the sense of the communication. Interruptions delay understanding and at times cause readers to lose a sense of the in-between, the inference, the connection. Multi-tasking interrupts and challenges what reading requires: memory, attention, a sense of space, an expectation, and a desire to know (Nass, 2010).

Students in their multimodal world are accustomed to the fusion of word-image-text. They are familiar with the quick text, message, clip, and the ability to manage several ongoing communications between many. They can collage like early 20th-century avant-garde artists. Multitasking and interruptions are the norm. Yet, reading a screen is not the same as reading a text. When viewing a composed frame, it is seen differently, as the eyes move among text, image, sound (if there), unbound by the lines. The eye moves about, seeing, the hand clicks, taps, the head positions itself to gaze, looking while doing other things.

A conflict exists between the linear world of print culture and non-linear world of multimodal discourse. Many students have internalized this conflict and the tension between these two worlds is palpable. The conflict is daily and also within teachers, administrators, and schools. Here's the vocal point of the problem: the education system is still rooted in the printed lined text. To advance, students must be able to read and write linear texts. Yet, multimodal discourse flourishes and is the dominant form of communication.

To prepare students for the world, it is necessary to address both within ourselves and in our classrooms. And in addressing both, there are some advantages: there is more room to explore and develop communication skills, aesthetics, and rhetoric. Students have real visual strengths and they can be used in a systematic way to foster language growth. In other words, educators can use one type of seeing to foster growth with another type of seeing. Reading is a certain kind of kind of visual work (Speer et al, 2009). Writing is a specific kind of visual exercise. When considering perception, there are at least three kinds at play in the ELA classroom: book perception, image perception, and social/commercial perception (Shivers et al, 2017). From the very beginning of the bound book, educators have fused together image and text.

By bringing these modals together in a ELA classroom, they automatically include more students and more aspect of their lived experience. Once reading is understood to be a visual exercise, other skills can be included and honed; similarly, if writing is a visual exercise, those skills can be improved. Understanding the principles of a multimodal discourse and visual poetics, educators can ask students to apply these principles themselves and further develop their publishing skills.

Classroom Practice

Given the cultural context inside and outside the classroom, a classroom practice that embraces aspects of multimodal discourse expands literacy in general and has very specific cognitive, emotional, and positive social results. Naturally, new skill sets arrive in the classroom as do new learning difficulties and educators contend with a constantly interrupted world.

For some students writing, reading, and/or speaking is a difficult, arduous, and discouraging process. Educators have the positive role of finding ways to foster communication and language growth. Below are a range of classroom practices from the quick five-minute warm-up to the longer major assignments. These practices are divided into three areas: Reading/Seeing, Writing/Marking, and Designing/Framing. The three domains of meaning are at the heart of generating a positive classroom workspace. Building a relationship with seeing, providing flexibility to meet curriculum expectations, and building confidence in new skills by using visual and media strengths to foster language growth establishes a space where reward, attention, and learning can grow (Adcock et al, 2005). These areas are constantly intertwined, but for the purposes of beginning a multimodal classroom practice, each area is explored individually.

Reading/Seeing

Foregrounding the process of seeing builds language skills; to spend time looking changes the perception. Students look, infer and discuss. Images communicate knowledge visually and appeal to the largest and earliest fully developed aspect of our brains. An educator who understands that an image communicates knowledge visually, then begins a classroom practice of observing, inferring, postulating. In the foundational Yale study, the use of the fine arts enhanced diagnostic skills building observational skills has multiple applications for various disciplines (Dolve, Friedlaendar, Braverman, 2001). Educators can begin to read images in the ELA classroom by spending time 'seeing' a picture.

Assignment. Choose an image from a notable, vetted collection from a museum online collection. Choose an image that has some representational features, and one that could be read in more than one way. Make sure everyone can see the image from their seat. Provide guidelines for the discussion. As a teacher, only ask follow-up questions. Let the students show what they see. Begin with observations: what do you see? Be sure to let everyone have a chance to speak either to the whole group or one on one. Do not correct the observations; rather ask for further explanation: explain how you see this. Don't favor one observation over another. Next, inferences: what do you think is going on in this image? Students will have much to say, so let them. But always ask, what makes you think this from what you see? The discussion will grow. Allow for the students to have different stories of what they see. This exercise can be practiced regularly and as the students become more fluent with the process, the time of seeing and discussion can be extended.

The first level of seeing only entails saying what is seen and using language (not pointing) to describe what is seen. Importantly, the teacher is only the facilitator here, not offering an interpretation, but asking questions of clarification. Next, the student articulates from the observation work, possible narratives or explanations. We began with representational images and then later in the year, explored all kinds of images, sculptures, and genres. Students will offer various 'readings' of the image and teachers should not run the interpretation, but provide time for students to revise, listen, re-look, discuss. The teacher's role here is to ask follow-up questions:

what do you observe that gives you this understanding of the image? When we read, we need space. Images can relate to course content, but the important aspect of what we are teaching is the process of seeing. As students become more confident and learn how to say what they see, the process of seeing becomes an aspect of knowing the world, others, and the self.

The seeing exercise can be directed to the whole class, in small groups, or one on one. The seeing is always a story of perception. So, when students are asked, 'what do you see?' the word 'see' is really what they perceive. Perception relates to stance, knowledge, assumptions, beliefs, experience (Shivers, Levenson, Tan, 2017). It is important to ask if something has been missed as it shows that all perspectives matter, that even a whole group can miss something, and anyone can see something others miss.

One of the more important aspects of reading is gaining independence and fostering readings that are based upon inquiry, not reporting for information. Leave the reading open to the class, to the individual student, whatever they come up with, they must support by textual evidence. A simple question of reading, 'what do you see'? is a question whereby educators begin to interact with the text within themselves, and then, if articulated, with others.

Both images and texts point, suggest, direct, the reading; following signs and beginning to infer. Images have components of composition, texts have time and sequence. The linear text follows lines. The image follows composed spaces. There is no argument that reading text is a good practice, and from this practice numerous other things occur.

Image work can begin simply using any image; however, the better the image, the more possibility for the student and classroom. Art is more rewarding to the brain than just a regular image (Lacey et al 2011). Most museums have online collections, so this is a good place to start since students have had little experience with the images that have shaped our culture. These images have been vetted and tested over time.

The Yale Center for British Art, for example, has an online collection accessible anywhere in the world, and many of the images are open source and can be used without a fee. The teacher can choose an image that would give the students an opportunity to have a closer look as well as being a good fit for the class. Asking what the student sees reveals how they perceive the world. By encouraging everyone to comment at some point and by asking follow-up questions, establishes a practice of looking and continued looking.

Letting the students know how long to practice provides duration and boundaries. The benefits are multiple: students use their visual cortex with their language; they see more as they look longer and learn not everything is immediate; and all students see something – therefore they can participate alleviating alienation or low self-confidence.

Student responses allow the educator to see the levels of articulation, the range of abilities to describe, the inability to be precise. If a student writes, 'tree' and another student writes, 'tall tree' and another student writes a tall green-gray tree with flowing limbs' the educator has insight into the student's ability to link the visual with the linguistic. This practice can be folded into reading: how the author describes the scene, what is seen through word choice; and later into writing.

Once a visual 'reading' practice is established, students begin to expand their perception to include what they sense as well as what they see. Just as in a text, educators can pick up tone with images. It is also possible to open up a conversation about stereotypes: this color means this emotion, the framing suggests this relationship, this physical stance suggests power. A seeing practice can be directed in many directions where each student learns how to articulate his/her visual experience.

Reading/seeing beyond the fine arts. Not all students have visited a museum and many have not spent a lot of time in front of a painting; however, students have seen hundreds of ads and have quite a bit of experience with the composition of the ad-world-view. Kilbourne (1999) argued that ads don't simply sell products they also sell a lifestyle. Issues of race, class, and gender, permeate the ad landscape. Interestingly, students often are unaware of the power of ad-world view until we start to look closely at the images.

Looking at the ad worldview, as Kress & Leeuwen (2001) have pointed out, there are different experiences with the direct or indirect gaze, with or without a border, the open or closed mouth. Looking upon one image or a collection of images allows an exploration of cultural assumptions of what it means to be a person. Ads are built to persuade, and designed to change, a person's behavior.

Assignment. People often do not see how an entire magazine contains a way of seeing the world. For the assignment, each student chooses his/her own magazine to analyze. The task is to first read the images as content and then ask observational questions: what is the world-view of body, position, language, stance, scene? To what extent do these images relate to the articles and other content of the magazine? How are these images used to portray a world-view, lifestyle, a stance? Based on these images, what are the needs, anxieties, concerns of the target audience?

In these assignments, students attend to what they see, investigate their perception, and build further awareness of the how meaning is made. At times, educators may direct the exercise as is sometimes done with reading a difficult text, but the educators' 'reading' and our 'seeing' should not be the only reading/seeing active in the classroom. Students will discover for themselves how images work and the more opportunities we provide to explore the mechanisms of visual meaning, the more opportunities we have to increase language growth.

Writing/Marking

It is important to incorporate the process of using a vocabulary of marking, seeing, and composing, as words to describe acts of understanding into the work of reading a text. Bartholomae & Petrosky (2002) argue for giving students material that is not completely controllable or 'clear', as well as providing texts that are not completely understandable. Too often, educators are afraid to give students texts that might be in places confusing or difficult. Consequently, students rarely experience the process of recognizing what they don't understand and figuring out how they might come to an understanding.

The reading process, then, becomes a noticing of what is not understood or is new to the horizon. The advantage for this practice for at-risk students, or students who have difficulties with the ELA curriculum, is that no one individual can claim they know everything –including the teacher; difficult aspects of the text are not ignored; each student goes through the process of understanding. Instead of being a fearful reader, the unknown, not understood, unclear aspects of the text become part of the process of learning.

Reading, then, is a dialogue between what is known and unknown, seen and unseen, understood and misunderstood and gives students space, allows them to not be anxious about getting it wrong, creates a level playing field in discussions, assignments, and presentations. The educator has an opportunity to build marking the text into their reading strategies by physically marking the text.

Readers have always marked texts and if looking at annotations historically, it is clear to see from the very beginning of books and manuscripts, comments, special marks, and colors, have been employed as acts of reading and comprehension. In other words, no matter what the method, style, or approach, all annotations are a visual record of the reading experience.

The point here is not a particular approach (each reader eventually figures out how to mark their own texts); but an agreement that just as texts affect the reader mentally, students can literally mark a text as the experience is processed. This act of marking the text can also transform into an aesthetic act and process (Shivers, et al 2017). Literally, seeing what is known and unknown, the text leaves the world of abstraction, as the reader works on it with words, images, colors, designs.

As with Latin texts without punctuation, a good reader knew when to note a change of pause and effect. Only in the past 100 years or so have footnotes been added. The word, para (beside) graph (mark) was a move to note when the sense of the writing changed. Indentation, like many stylistic devices, is a creation of reading experience into a visual domain: periods, question marks, colons, semi-colons, indentations, footnotes, etc. have all been added to the page. Too often these markers are treated as some fixed absolute true throughout all time. As Parkes (1992, 2016) argues, the visual design of text continually morphs.

Annotations then become another act of seeing and re-reading then becomes a memory of understanding/not-understanding. Educators count as valuable the reader's process of understanding and misunderstanding. When educators think of the range of students in front of them, they build various practices that promote ways of meaning making to the reading task.

Assignment. Here is one method that embraces multiple aspects of the reading experience. Any article or length of article will do. As the student reads, they are asked to highlight the text in four areas with different colors: new, difficult, confusing, interesting. Add to the margin a brief written note explaining why. The annotation is not a process of agreeing or disagreeing with the text. Rather, the reader marks his/her own experience of process visually on the page. Once the work is completed the teacher can 'see' what the student experienced while reading. This method works for all levels of readers and can be differentiated to fit each particular reading need. Once the visual work is completed the multimodal text can be used for conversation, writing, and/or designing.

Seeing/Drawing

Accepting images as texts to be read, opens up many ways to build confidence, learn to develop a sense of time and place, build attention stamina, links active seeing with verbal expression and dialogue. Viewing and then drawing an image in an English class takes active seeing into the domain of writing as a form of discovery. Bringing to the page what is seen via drawing, following a practice of attention by writing, and discovering new ways of seeing, sharpens students' observation and inference skills, and joins them in the meaning-making process.

Helen Cixous in her "Talking Liberties" interview with the BBC says that picking up a pencil is one of the most powerful acts an individual can have. Educators see the value of working with an image in discussions about what students see. Another way to build a practice of seeing is to draw images, and then write about the image in a variety of ways, and thus to think about drawing as a way of thinking and writing (Ernst, 1994).

The point is to bring the image in the room, give the students a piece a paper, and have them draw what they see. The act of drawing is also an act of building attention. Students are not graded by their accuracy, or skill as artists; rather, their work is a work of making marks on a page as a way to interact with the image that they see. As the school year progresses, the acts of drawing can take many forms.

Assignment. Part One. How does the process work? First, the teacher also draws and is an active participant --- as much as possible. Begin with some description on the benefits of the process: focused attention, developing observation and perception skills, and self/world awareness. Begin with a very complicated print like Albert Durer's Melencolia I (1514), and one that is more or less realistic, and only give them about 10 minutes to draw. Ask the students to draw some aspect of what they see; let them choose. The room is quiet. No phones. Everyone draws. No judgement. Some students will say, 'I can't draw'. The teacher reassures them that's not a problem and the task is simply to draw what you see. As the year progresses, the students draw for longer stretches of time with various directions: to draw the whole image, draw a section, or an object within the image and the continued, draw what you see. For examples, see the blog, A Closer Look.

Students are not required to share their drawings - some sharing happens naturally, as with a neighbor. However, no student is required to share in front of the class. Later in the year, as the class grows into a community of listening, dialogue and respect, the teacher can open up a time for sharing and many will.

The image itself is not viewed as a piece of information. Although the image history, genre, and cultural significance is important, the task is participating in visual acts of knowing. The teacher's responsibility is to make good choices, to find images that work with the students enrolled in class. Of course, the teacher can link the images to the content of the course and this can expand their experience in a particular unit or lesson; nevertheless, the main point is to follow the line of another artist, other interpretations of the world, other visual makers. The students step into this process themselves and begin to make marks on the page. In some situations, students can have journals (without lines) they use for the year. This allows them to see how their own work develops over the year. In other situations, if journals are not an option, a teacher can use paper and have folder for each student. Both options work.

Part Two: Marking has two sides: visual and linguistic. After the drawing comes the writing. The teacher provides these prompts and lets the students choose: describe what you see, tell the story of the image, open invitation to any writing. The pacing is similar to the drawing: if students draw for ten minutes, then they can write for ten minutes. As their stamina and interest grow from the benefit of the practice, the times for drawing and writing expand. Regardless of the time, the two acts are always linked. The writing aspect of the process is rooted in the goal of having students write without worry of being corrected, or having to format a page according to a rubric, or have the purpose of the exercise to create a report.

Writing itself is transformative. And since writing is a skill, the more students practice, the more fluency they have. The job of the educator is to frame the activity, keep students on task, and validate the process by taking part in the process. Once the routine is established, the students begin to benefit from the acts of attention in drawing and the acts of attention in writing. Like the commonplace book tradition, students literally start building a working notebook and join a vast and beautiful tradition. The role of journal/working notebook in the Arts and the Sciences is a well-established phenomenon.

Learning the language of seeing and writing. Not all students embrace the process. Some students have said they didn't like the drawing at first, but later did. Importantly, the goal of the drawing is not to make realistic copies of the images. The drawing allows students to start thinking about what they see and how to frame a composition on the page. Indirectly, they learn about perspective, rule of thirds, tone, foreground, background, etc. Sometime during the year, once the practice is established, the teacher could show ways of reading compositions and the elemental components such as contrast, perspective as ways visual rhetoric works. The educator understands the purpose of the activity: students focus on the visual world and then use that visual world to create linguistic and visual meaning. In the words of one struggling student, 'by drawing, I can see better when we read. I can imagine the story better because I have been practicing'. Conceptual knowledge is organized visually (Kan et al, 2003) and here the student has linked seeing and drawing with understanding.

Designing/Framing

Each of these areas are related: seeing, drawing, writing. When educators embrace these practices in the ELA classroom they open up more room for all kinds of learners, and students at all levels. Providing emotional, cognitive, and creative space for students to explore and giving room for different kinds of learners makes the whole class stronger and more engaged.

Most texts in school are multimodal. So, students are accustomed to view a page with graphs, visuals, and illustrations. In fact, the books have always had a visual, illustrated component. Yet, often in the ELA curriculum multimodal texts are not used, sought after or required reading. Books like *The Books of Books* (Lommen, 2012), *Beautiful Evidence* (Tufte, 2006), *Cover to Cover* (LaPlantz, 1995), *The Book of Trees* (Lima, 2014), *The Art of Illumination* (Husband, 2008) and *Understanding Comics* (McCloud, 1993) easily provides teachers with the necessary background to show how the page has been and is being designed, illustrated, and composed.

In the day to day acts of communication, writing is often illustrated, framed, and designed to create an overall effect. So many students practice this or experience this on a regular, daily basis in their various social media accounts. What they don't always know is that the grammar behind these technologies has been in play for a long time.

Students begin the school year practicing seeing and drawing at a basic level; additionally, students annotate texts. Students also analyze how images persuade and communicate visually and linguistically. These practices can grow in complexity and are easily differentiated.

Assignment. This assignment can be done with any writing prompt. But, using it at the end of a unit or as the final prompt provides more options. The final writing project for the year can be a collection of writings, drawings, and annotations. The final essay, which would incorporate course content, could easily be illustrated. For example, the required essay is illustrated from some element created/used during the year. Students design the page to create additional meaning from the writing. Alternatively, a student could create a new illustration. The act of reading an image is different than reading a text. Design allows these two worlds, one strictly linear and one non-linear, to mingle creating a third multimodal discourse. Software programs provide a host of design possibilities from fonts, margins, color to text box, shapes, clips, and images. Although some students can get (and have) carried away with artifice, nevertheless, most students find a way to accept the design as a vital part of communication. One requirement of the essay is to explain how the design enhances the communication.

As students become more confident in reading and seeing the effects of visual rhetoric, we should ask them to produce this rhetoric within their own work. How might you illustrate the essay to extend, support, and expand your argument? Avant-garde poetics teaches us page design is cultural and the page is a space of exploration to further communicate. Form always tells a story (Perloff, 1991).

Framing

We have been framing images for some time, which means we are accustomed to having an inside and an outside. The printed photograph is a visual page. Since the birth of the photographic image in the early 19th century, educators see that they must select and choose what is framed. It is impossible to take a picture of the whole world. The image-machine exists in the world, occupying space.

Now, many students carry their cell phones with them and often use their camera phones to tell jokes, convey messages, make a point, or to be humorous. Educators can use this practice as a way to build critical and creative awareness; asking students to use the camera as a way of interpreting their experience of school by asking them to think visually about their experience. If they can only take one picture of the school, what would they take? To complete this task, they have to reconsider their daily experience of the building.

Students must take an image that represents the way they feel or think about their experience. The results range from the quick stereotype to the well thought out photo. When educators also complete the assignment (not necessary to show the students, but rather to go through the experience), they gain a sense of the critical faculties needed to perform the task.

Assignment. Take a picture of the school that tells a story or offers an interpretation of your experience of school. Show the picture in class, present. What is the thesis? What is the argument being made? Discussion.

Students presented their images in class and the class discussed how the image made a visual argument. In the next slide, they present their linguistic thesis, followed by a slide with the image and thesis side by side. The class discusses if the visual and linguistic arguments are compatible, incongruent, ambiguous and/or in dialogue with each other.

In many ways, all of these activities are the basis for the combination of image-sound-text. Slide presentations take the fixed object of an image/page and link it to sequence. Additionally, slides can contain text, image, video, and sound. Slideshows use the very same grammar as cinema. The slide as a page that can be composed with multimodal texts. And now, we can consider sequence as we would in an argument (Duarte, 2008). Too many slide presentations lack creativity or awareness of how visual rhetoric works. Far too often, educational presentations are filled with text, barely visible, and more like a handout.

The PechaKucha 20X20 (Klein & Dytham, 2003) movement shows that presentations are a form of art. By expecting students to be creative and innovative, it gives students the opportunity to use their visual media skills to foster critical and creative insights. Linking together book, image, and social perception provides students with the opportunity to use their strengths to enhance their difficulties. Additionally, by analyzing commercials and film, students can begin to see how moving images work. Slide by slide, frame by frame, working a point with visual effect. Students have the capacity to make images, and make moving images. Giving them the opportunity to make a point by how they film something, how they photograph something, gives them the opportunity to use their visual strengths to make a critical argument. In one assignment, students have to take two photos as a response to the question, 'what have I learned?, what do I want to say?. The image must speak for itself. Yet, in the notes, they explain their work.

Think of framing as a meaning maker. Think of the camera as a way to show a point. Think of filming behind the snap, the quick cat video as a process of sequence. Think of the phone-photo-machine as a new alphabetic technology that can be applied in multiple directions.

Conclusion

Reading and writing effectively are life skills. As ELA teachers, we need to seek to understand why and how students find writing, readings, and speaking difficult. We must also not ignore our students daily and life experience of communication. Multimodal discourse is the dominant form of discourse, yet ELA classrooms have had a difficult time incorporating the grammar behind this discourse. Reading and seeing are linked to perception and understanding. Drawing and writing are linked to spatial organization and social connections. We see, we hear, we speak, we act. Given that our students are developing these skills, we should use them all that we can so students can find a way to negotiate the world, the self, and others.

By addressing large aspects of who students are and honoring their experience, we open more possibilities of creative and critical language growth. Understanding that meaning is linear and non-linear, linguistic and visual, gives the teacher more ways to address the needs of the students in the classroom. A student who can draw an intricate interpretation of a scene from a text in twenty minutes, but has difficulties writing more than a few sentences in the same amount of time has true strengths. Instead of saying, the student just can't write we should say, look what the student can do with the pencil. Both acts of the pencil are readings of the text. More than one student has exclaimed, 'I like English now'.

A willingness to explore how a student communicates, a willingness to explore multimodal discourse, does provide more space for all learners. Once a student realizes space exists for them, they feel relief, peace, intrigue, and over the year, their confidence in themselves, in their ways of reading and writing, grows. Although still there, the formal demands culturally at play remain. The practices do not run from rigor or the demand for quality, but by practicing visual literacy and skills in the ELA classroom, students produce more engaged work, are more aware of how meaning is made, and have more practice making meaning. The same is true in the world.

As noted in Adam Grant's *Originals: How Non-Conformists Move the World*, a study of Nobel Prize winners showed the remarkable effect of using many of these practices in daily life. "But the Nobel Prize winners were dramatically more likely to be involved in the arts than less accomplished scientists" (2016 p. 46). In fact, drawing increased the odds by seven times, while writing poetry twelve times among those with similar qualifications. These practices discussed above keep us all open to the unexpected surprise, while developing the ability to attend, see, hear, and listen. Of course, these practices are not a magic pill and are not enough on their own to promote language growth or heal the troubles of having difficulties in an ELA classroom. Classroom teachers who listen, who attend to the changes in culture and parents who take the time to find ways forward, are still very much in demand as are administrators who don't shy away from the necessary flexibility and understanding needed for schools to care for children.

Points to Remember

- *Students have visual strengths and a range of visual experiences that can be a starting point for language growth.*
- *Aspects of the ELA curriculum generate anxiety in students who have low performance or difficulties with the material.*
- *The conflict between linear and non-linear modes of communication can be internalized by the student, teacher, and/or the curriculum.*
- *Focusing, seeing, drawing, and presenting develop the skills of attention, cognitive/emotional growth, and creativity.*
- *Seeing/writing, drawing/reading are linked.*
- *Visual literacy skills and practices build creative and critical language growth.*

- *Multimodal discourse should be read, produced, and discussed in all ELA classes and be a part of the K-12 curriculum.*
- *All classrooms at all levels have students with a range of reading, writing, speaking levels and benefit from visual literacy practices.*
- *The teachers should do the assignments they give.*

Author's note: Thanks to the following teachers and administrators who provided feedback on the design and nature of the chapter: Carol Blejwas, Teacher, Hall High School, West Hartford, CT; Jordon Schmitzer, Teacher, CREC Public Safety Academy, Enfield CT; Kelly Price, ELA Curriculum Specialist, CREC, Hartford CT; Tina Mirto, Curriculum Specialist, CREC Museum Academy, Bloomfield, CT. Thanks also to the Department of Education at The Yale Center for British Art for their programs, continued support, and collaboration.

References

Adcock, A. R., Thangavel, A., Whitfield-Gabrieli, S., Knutson, B., Gabrieli, J.D.E., Reward- *Motivated Learning: Mesolimbic Activation Precedes Memory Formation, Neuron Volume* 50, Issue 3, 2006, Pages 507-517, ISSN 0896-6273http://dx.doi.org/10.1016/j.neuron.2006.03.036.

Bartholomae, D., & Petrosky, T. (2002). *Ways of reading: An anthology for writers* (6th ed.). Boston: Bedford/St. Martins.

Dolev, J.C., Friedlaender, L.K., Braverman, I.M. *Use of fine art to enhance visual diagnostic skills.* DOI:10.1001/jama.286.9.1019

Ernst, K. (1994). *Picturing learning: Artists & writers in the classroom.* Portsmouth, NH: Heinemann.

Grant, A. (2016). *Originals: how non-conformists move the world.* New York: Penguin Books.

Husband, T.B. (2008). *The Art of illumination: The Limbourg brothers and the belles heures of Jean de France, Duc de Berry.* New York: The Metropolitan Museum of Art; New Haven,CT: Yale University Press.

Kan, I. P., Barsalou, L. W., Solomon, K. O., Minor, J. K., & Thompson-Schill, S. L. (2003). Role of mental imagery in a property verification task: fMRI evidence for perceptual representations of conceptual knowledge. *Cognitive Neuropsychology,* 20(3-6), 525-540.doi:10.1080/02643290244000257

Klein, A. Dytham, M. (2003- present). *PechaKucha: 20 images x 20 seconds.* Retrieved from http://www.pechakucha.org/

Kilbourne, J. (1999). *Deadly persuasion: Why women and girls must fight the addictive power of advertising.* New York, NY: Free Press.

Kress, G., & Van Leeuwen, T. (2001). *Multimodal discourse: The modes and media of contemporary communication.* New York, NY: Oxford University Press.

Lacey, S., Hagtvedt, H., Patrick V. M., Anderson, A., Stilla, R., Deshpande, G., Hu, X., Sato, J.R., Reddy, S., Sathian, K. *Art for reward's sake: Visual art recruits the ventral striatum.*Retrieved from https://www.ncbi.nlm.nih.gov/pubmed/21111833

LaPlantz, S. (1995). *Cover to Cover: Creating techniques for making beautiful books, journals, & albums.* Asheville, NC: Lark Books.

Lindemann, E. (2001). *A rhetoric for writing teachers* (4th ed.). New York, NY: Oxford FreePress.

Lommen, M. (Ed.) (2012). *The book of books: 500 hundred years of graphic innovation.* New York, NY: Thames & Hudson.

McCloud, S. (1993). *Understanding comics: the invisible art.* New York, NY: HarperCollins.

Nass, Clifford (2010). Interview. In Rushkoff & Dretzen writers, R Dretzin (director). Feb 02, 2010. In Digital Nation: Life on the virtual frontier. *Frontline. PBS.* Interview Retrieved from http://www.pbs.org/wgbh/pages/frontline/digitalnation/interviews/nass.html

Parkes, M. (1992). *Pause and effect: An introduction to the history of punctuation in the West.* Berkeley, CA: University of California Press.

Perloff, M. (1991). *Radical artifice: writing poetry in the age of media.* Chicago, IL: University of Chicago Press.

Rideout, V. J., Foehr, U.G., & Roberts, R.F. (2010). *Generation M2: Media in the lives of 8 to 18 year olds.* Retrieved from http://www.kff.org/other/report/generation-m2-media-in-the-lives-of-8-to-18-year-olds/

Rushkoff, D & Dretzin, R (writers), Rachel Dretzin (Director & Producer). Feb 02, 2010. Digital

Nation: Life on the virtual frontier. *Frontline. PBS.* Retrieved from http://www.pbs.org/wgbh/pages/frontline/digitalnation/

Shivers, J., Levenson, C., & Tan, M. (2017). Visual Literacy, creativity and the teaching of argument. Learning Disabilities. *A Contemporary Journal,* 15(1), 67-84. Retrieved fromhttps://eric.ed.gov/?id=EJ1141995

Speer, N. K., Reyonlds, J.R., Swallow, K.M., & Zacks, J.M (2009). Reading stories activates neural representations of visual and motor experiences. *Psychological Science,* 20 (8), 989-999. DOI:10.1111/j.1467-9280.2009.02397

Tufte, E. (2006). *Beautiful evidence.* Cheshire, CT: Graphics Press LCC.

Yale Center for British Art (n.d.). Online Collection. Retrieved fromhttp://britishart.yale.edu/collections/using-collections/online-collections

Chapter 6

Understanding Student and Teacher Behaviors from Two Perspectives: A Schema for Success in Teaching Students with Learning and Behavioral Challenges

Vance L. Austin, *Manhattanville College*

As the inclusive classroom, together with its instructional corollary, response to intervention (RTI), continues to develop into standard practice throughout the United States, classroom teachers can no longer claim students with special needs and behavioral challenges are not their responsibilities. Frequently, within the inclusion model, special and general educators are paired to serve students with a variety of needs – gifted, average, learning disabled, and emotionally disturbed, in a single classroom. As a result, all teachers must now acquire the skills and dispositions necessary to effectively teach students with diverse learning and behavioral requirements. Teacher preparation programs and schools must find ways to ensure that preservice and novice teachers are prepared to address the increasingly diverse needs of all students assigned to their classrooms. In discussing the needs of some of our most challenging students, Cavin (1998) encourages teachers to,

> …remember that these kids with all of their problems, their criminal records, their probation officers, their idiosyncrasies, their unlovable characteristics, and their strange families are still kids. They need someone to care. They need someone to accept them. They need to know they are somebody. If you are willing to provide these ideals, you can be the connection that bridges the gap from drop-out to diploma. (p. 10)

A further incentive to stay the course with challenging students was provided by a former colleague who observed, "for some kids, these days in school may be the best of their lives: the safest, the happiest, and the most secure." The author never forgot this insightful pronouncement and it helped change his attitude about teaching even the most oppositional, defiant students.

A final inducement to persevere with the challenges presented by students with learning and behavioral problems comes from data provided by the U.S. Office of Juvenile Justice. In 2010, according to their records, 70,792 juveniles were incarcerated in the U.S., the greatest number worldwide. In fact, the incarceration rate for juveniles (school-age children) in the U.S.

in 2002 was 336 for every 100,000 youth - compare that figure to the country with the next highest rate, South Africa, with 69 of every 100,000 youth in detention (as cited in Mendel, 2011).

In response to these abysmal statistics and his own extensive experience, DeMuro (2010), the former commissioner of the Pennsylvania Juvenile Corrections system, describes the current state of juvenile justice in the U.S. as "iatrogenic" (preventable harm introduced by the caregiver, in this case, the juvenile justice system) (as cited in Mendel, 2011). Mendel (2011) notes further that while education and treatment at most juvenile detention facilities is nonexistent, the average annual cost to house an incarcerated youth in a detention facility is approximately $88,000; whereas, the cost to provide that same individual with effective intervention services in a public or specialized school is approximately $10,000. Moreover, the recidivism rate for incarcerated youth in New York State, for example, three years or more after release, ranges from 73-89 percent (Annie E. Casey Foundation, 2011).

Similarly, a 2006 investigation revealed that only 33 percent of youth released from a

Pennsylvania corrections camp program who said they would return to school did so (Hjalmarsson, 2008). Since there are, effectively, no rehabilitation programs in most juvenile corrections facilities, youths detained in them can become more antisocial and more inclined to engage in criminal behaviors after their release. Thus, the data clearly suggests that the last, best hope for most of these at-risk youth is in school, and perhaps the best models of prosocial behavior are their teachers.

Is teaching (pedagogy) most appropriately understood as Art, Science, or Craft? This question stirs up the tenets of a very old debate, effectively described in N. L. Gage's book, *The Scientific Basis of the Art of Teaching* (1978). In that book, Gage defined pedagogy as "...any activity on the part of one person intended to facilitate learning on the part of another" (p. 14). Given the focus of this chapter, which concerns the education of students with learning and behavioral differences in today's K-12 schools, I think we need a more inclusive definition. Specifically, one that acknowledges that teaching has been transformed in the 21st century to incorporate a more expansive job description: today's educator serves as a role model for prosocial behavior, provides examples of civil discourse, and, in some cases, acts as a surrogate parent.

Readers only need to examine the changing social structure that surrounds our children; specifically, the unstable economy, which determines how we live in society and has required a radical increase in the number of hours spent working, and has thus all but eliminated the "stay-at-home" parent to understand this radical change. Absent parental guidance, many American students have found themselves without the traditional role model who once taught and reinforced prosocial behaviors and discouraged antisocial ones.

So then, back to the original question about the qualification of teaching, Gage (1978) suggested that, rather than teaching being considered an art or science, it should be, in its highest form, considered an amalgam of both. According to the Cambridge Dictionary Online (2012) the term "pedagogy" is imprecisely defined as: "...the study of the methods and activities of teaching." Essentially, the word denotes the skills that constitute effective, systematized instruction. There is no shortcut to attaining this vital skill set, which is really honed and refined throughout the professional lifetime of the teacher. Frankly, if educators do not know how to teach subject matter or impart knowledge about a topic or skill, it matters little that they have much to teach and possess a vast knowledge base. Most educators know of individuals who are recognized widely for their expertise in a subject, but do not possess the pedagogical skills to effectively impart that knowledge to others.

Undeniably, sound pedagogical skills must be acquired through effective training, a reflective practice, and a more reflective practice that can be nurtured (Loughran, 2002). Ideally, a teacher's pedagogical skills should constantly develop as the teacher gains experience and hones these skills through a commitment to effective professional development. Palmer (1998) asserts further, that "...good teaching cannot be reduced to techniques; good teaching comes from the identity and integrity of the teacher" (p. 10). In a more expansive view, the author would propose that, like Gage (1978), effective teaching and effective teachers must possess a "scientific basis" for teaching that is construed as an expertise in the subject matter as well as the passion that is integral to an "artistic" pedagogy, but would here add the facility to build relationships with students. This enlarged characterization is delineated in the author's "framework for good teaching," which follows.

A New Archetype of Teacher Pedagogy

Cogill (2008) states that pedagogy, as it pertains to the teaching profession, is multi-faceted and thus difficult to simply define. Nevertheless, Watkins and Mortimer (1999) describe the term as "any conscious activity by one person designed to enhance the learning of another" (p. 3) - note the similarity in this definition and the one proposed by Gage (1978). Alexander (2003), expands on this definition by adding, "It is what one needs to know, and the skills one needs to command in order to make and justify the many different kinds of decisions of which teaching is constituted" (p. 3).

Suggesting that teacher knowledge is integral to pedagogy, Cogill (2008) cites Shulman's (1987) seven categories as a schema for understanding the nuanced term. This "framework" is very helpful in understanding pedagogical skills as they pertain to the teaching profession. They include: (a) content knowledge, (b) general pedagogical knowledge [e.g., classroom control, group work], (c) pedagogical content knowledge [simply understood as "content or subject knowledge"], (d) curriculum knowledge, which is more specific to instructional design, (e) knowledge of learners and their characteristics, (f) knowledge of educational contexts [e.g., schools and their communities], and (g) knowledge of education purposes and their values [for students] (as cited in Cogill, 2008, p. 1-2). Simply put, pedagogy is the "how to" in effectively imparting a skill to another.

In a different vein, Korthagen (2004) posits a developmental model of pedagogical skills central to a good teacher. He refers to this model as "the onion" because the skills are equally important and interrelated. They flow from a central mission, through identity [of the teacher], beliefs [of the teacher], competencies [teaching], behaviors [relative to effective teaching], and, finally, the interaction of the teacher's environment with the teacher and her instruction. In line with his model, Korthagen (2004) proposes a holistic educator development, one that finds a middle ground between humanistic and behaviorist perspectives. He further urges that the teacher educator understand her own core qualities to more effectively and authentically promote them in her prospective teachers. Ostensibly, these prospective teachers would reciprocate in reflecting on their "core qualities" and values to encourage the development of these qualities within their own students.

In a similar way, Palmer (1998) insists that good teachers know themselves (i.e., "identity"), and are honest with themselves and others, unafraid to show their students and colleagues who they really are (i.e., "integrity") (p. 10). Loughran (2002) adds that teaching, in its highest form, requires an understanding of oneself and others and is predicated on the quality of relationship between the teacher and student. Many students with learning and behavioral challenges have had to acquire a heightened sensitivity to duplicity and the insincere, for the preservation of their emotional, and sometimes physical well-being. Teachers who are consistent, fair, and authentic are preferred by these students and thus are more apt to achieve success in teaching them (Austin et al., 2011).

Sound teacher pedagogy requires a "purpose," which establishes the starting point for learning; thus, the most effective teacher pedagogies involve the modeling of a desired skill, behavior, or disposition by a capable teacher to demonstrate the "why" or purpose of teaching a desired skill or conveying an idea. However, Loughran (2002) asserts that knowing "why" we teach must be linked to knowing "how" we [effectively] teach.

Northfield and Gunstone (1997) articulate six recommendations for the development of a sound pedagogy that are especially relevant to novice and preservice teachers. They are as follows: (1) prospective teachers have needs that must be considered in planning and implementing a program and these change through their pre-service development; (2) the transition from learner to teacher is difficult but is aided by working closely with one's peers; (3) the student teacher is a learner who is actively constructing views of teaching and learning based on personal experiences strongly shaped by perceptions held before entering the program; (4) the teaching/learning approaches advocated in the program should be modeled by the teacher educators in their own practice;

(5) student-teachers should see the preservice program as an educational experience of worth; and (6) preservice education programs are inevitably inadequate (it is the start of a teacher's career that will involve appreciably more learning over time).

Schön's (1983) conception of the reflective practitioner is an essential notion for those who teach in a preservice program, as well as for those learning to teach. In support of this contention, Sellars (2013) and Russell (1997) stress that an important aspect of sound pedagogy is self-reflection; that is, reflecting on one's teaching.

Smith (2012) and Noddings (2005) asserts that pedagogy is a process that consists of accompanying learners, caring for and about them, and bringing learning into their lives. Sound pedagogy, he continues, induces change in the learner and, ultimately, in the world. Thus, emerges the notion of "social pedagogy" in a revised definition suggested earlier in this chapter by Watkins and Mortimore (1999); to reiterate, "any conscious activity by one person designed to enhance learning in another" (p. 3). The authors add that teachers (and their pedagogies) are influenced by their contexts, i.e. students' learning differences and preparedness, the subject matter, their own prejudices and predispositions, likes and dislikes (refer to "attachment theory").

They must present their curriculums in different ways to address the social-emotional make-up (context) of the class (students), sequence of lessons, and knowledge of both learning groups and individuals (p. 6). Teachers, as pedagogues, help students see themselves as active agents contributing to their own learning, members of a community of learners engaged in the generation and evaluation of knowledge alongside the teacher (Watkins & Mortimore, 1999, p. 7-8).

In another, related direction, Friere (1970) and later, Bruner (1996) insisted that, to truly develop an effective pedagogical framework, the teacher must understand her cultural context as well as those of her students and how culture influences how and what one teaches. Alexander (2004) stated that [teacher] pedagogy may be understood as (a) what we need to know, (b) the skills needed to impart that knowledge, and (c) the commitment we need to display to make the many kinds of decisions required of a teacher each day. Children are engaged from very early on to make sense of their world.

The teacher's pedagogical imperative is to facilitate that natural process by helping children and adolescents make connections between new and familiar situations, directing student focus, piquing the interest and curiosity of the child, supporting all attempts to learn, structuring students' experiences, regulating levels of complexity and difficulty for them, and motivating them through success and acceptance. Expert teachers know the structure of their disciplines and this knowledge intersects with and enhances their pedagogical skills (Alexander, 2004).

Mascolo (2009) suggests that there are many experiential ways that teachers can develop their pedagogical skills; namely, (a) through their own practice, (b) through collaboration with colleagues, (c) through professional development opportunities, and (d) from the various extra-curricular roles they play (e.g., youth group worker, coach, parent, community club organizer).

As far back as 1896, a didactic model of teaching was encouraged: the heretofore "revolutionary" idea that teachers should share their knowledge with everyone (Comenius as cited in Gundem, 1992). Furthermore, Alexander (2004) contends that [teacher] pedagogues reflect on fundamental questions of life such as: "how should one live one's life? what is the right way to act in each situation? what does happiness consist of for me and others? how should I relate to others? and what sort of society should I be working towards?" (p. 11).

What is Known About Effective Pedagogy

An effective teacher pedagogy should (a) be clear about its goals, (b) have high expectations for students and provide them with motivation to learn, (c) incorporate beneficial technologies, and (d) be grounded in a well-tested theory, which inspires innovative practices (Ireson, Mortimore, & Hallam, 1999, p. 213). The authors also cite Vygotsky's (1987) notion of "cultural tools" and suggest that they might be relevant to our understanding of a "pedagogical framework." To that end, they suggest six fundamental ideas:

- Defining pedagogy. The term "pedagogy" is seldom clearly defined (or understood). It refers to teaching methods and concepts.

- No one-size-fits-all pedagogy. Some books on pedagogy have misinterpreted the term and have confused it with "teaching techniques" of which there are legions, and he concedes that many of these are effective, given the right contexts and the "right" students. It has also been defined in much broader philosophical terms to include a way of thinking about teaching and learning that involves self-reflection on the part of the teacher and a willingness to learn about, care for, and connect with her students. Rather than a "toolbox" of teaching strategies, the writer's approach has been to suggest a pedagogical framework, which can be applied broadly to enhance the effectiveness of any teaching initiative.

- Teachers are important. Good teachers, empowered by a sound pedagogy, are essential to inspiring learners to want to learn and in building their self-efficacy.

- Context matters. Transferable skills, those that are invaluable to the individual regardless of the context, are critical to students' success in school and in the world of work (Bolles, 2015). Examples of these include what we refer to generally as "social skills," e.g., knowing how to begin and end a conversation, how to be courteous and considerate of others' feelings, when to be silent and when to speak up, how to identify the "hidden curriculum" in a new social milieu and so on. In short, a teacher's pedagogy must include the provision of "real world" instruction in authentic contexts.

- Pedagogical principles. Derived from an analysis of many related articles on the subject. Included in these are the following:
    - Be clear about your goals and ensure that your students know them
    - Plan, organize, and manage your teaching effectively
    - Hold your students accountable to the highest expectations appropriate for them as individuals
    - Provide positive formative feedback to all your students
    - Address individual differences and needs in the inclusive classroom
    - Provide meaningful learning tasks that are informed by good assessment procedures
    - Teach "transferable skills" to all your students

- - Make your rules explicit and meaningful and don't forget to teach students how to acquire the "hidden curriculum" embedded in all social contexts
  - Teach students to identify their strengths and weaknesses as a means of empowerment and to take increasing responsibility for their own learning
  - Motivate and enthuse learners
- Acknowledge the fact that teachers are learners too. Cultivate a love of learning and bring your enthusiasm and passion for learning into the classroom.

Attachment Theory and Its Relevance for Teachers

Simply stated, "attachment theory" is promulgated by the belief that good teaching involves knowledge, pedagogy, and relationship. This last aspect of good teaching is often dealt with in teacher preparation programs through a course in classroom management techniques built upon the principles of contingency maintenance. Teachers are taught to reinforce good behavior and punish bad behavior; nevertheless, a relationship, even between student and teacher, involves a recursive interplay of forces affecting the development of both the student and the teacher. The goal is to help teachers by increasing their knowledge of the genesis of students' maladaptive behaviors as well as their own and, in this sense, the approach can appropriately be understood as applied psychodynamics in the classroom.

Being able to reflect upon our own behavior and that of another creates a state of "mindfulness" that reduces the possibility of reactive behaviors on the part of teachers. In more traditional psychodynamic theory, the approach might be called the transference and counter-transference between students and teachers. Since teachers are authority figures, students can easily "transfer" their conflicts with authority from the past onto teachers and make them conform to how students think about their world. Teachers, on the other hand, also bring to the relationship their own unresolved conflicts and familial and cultural influences and may misinterpret a child's behavior based on previous unresolved conflicts and losses.

Attachment theory challenges teachers to acknowledge the influence of their own parents and unique cultural milieu on their interpretation of the formation, function, and intentionality of the maladaptive behaviors exhibited by their students. It suggests that from early experiences with the primary attachment figure, the child develops an attachment style. There is much discussion as to whether teachers can be considered attachment figures. It is clear, however, that children bring their attachment style into the classroom and this interacts with the teacher's own attachment style, which allows for an interplay of relational dynamics that, if not properly understood, will only lead to poor classroom management. Students can be difficult because of emotional and behavioral disorders, many of which have as a major contributor the child's attachment style.

Bowlby (1958) posited that significant disruptions in the mother-child relationship were a predictor for subsequent psychopathology. However, more than just understanding attachment styles and being better able to manage difficult behaviors, there is also the question of whether teachers can be influential in changing the attachment styles of the children they interact with daily. In addition, if teachers are willing to critically examine their unique family and cultural influences, this self-awareness may help them appreciate the effects of behavioral influences of family and culture on their students. This metacognitive awareness may help teachers avoid projecting their own culturally situated prejudices and expectations onto their students, many of whom do not share the teacher's cultural perspective.

Inclusion, "Difference," and a Relevant Pedagogical Schema

Similarly, for those who teach students with disabilities, teacher pedagogy is centrally about the relevance of teaching to difference and diversity (Corbett & Norwich, 1999). Corbett and Norwich (1999) insist that teaching students with special education needs, requires the adoption of a "connective pedagogy", which describes the process of relating to individual learners with SEN with an acute awareness of and connection to the students' social context (p. 117). The authors further contend that differences between children might call for differences in the pedagogical "style" employed by these teachers. They continue that the teacher's pedagogy needs to be considered in terms of relationships and balances between practices that are (a) common to all students, (b) specific to some, and (c) unique to individuals.

Corbett and Norwich (999) address the question of why a teacher would feel called to become a "special educator" (p. 119). They suggest that it might be because the teacher relates to the students' vulnerabilities by connecting to their own. Thus, these "special" educators may possess an innate, "caring pedagogy", which is more individually sensitive (p. 125). Finally, Corbett and Norwich (1999) challenge teachers of students with special education needs, especially those working in the increasingly popular inclusive classrooms, to employ what they describe as a "connective pedagogy" to facilitate the development of a rapport with these students and help them develop a sense of "belongingness" with their classmates (p. 132).

One population of students that elicits concern in teachers, especially those considered novices, is the subgroup diagnosed with emotional disorders. In recent years, school districts across the country have reported an increased number of students classified with emotional and behavioral disorders (Office of Special Education Programs, 2006). To remain current and viable, teacher preparation programs and professional development staff in schools must begin to evaluate the qualities that effective classroom teachers demonstrate, even when confronted by the most challenging students, and which of the identified qualities can be acquired by less skilled or experienced teachers.

Becoming a Master Teacher

It is difficult to find research that distinguishes the universally recognized characteristics of a "master teacher." Most of what we read in journals and online listservs and blogs simply reflects the subjective opinions or insights of the author with very little, if any, scientific basis. This may be because the characteristics of acknowledged "master teachers" are germane to each. Therefore, absent a scientific criterion, the writer offers several lists of behaviors that are evident in most teachers that are recognized as exemplary. Teachers who wish to achieve this status must be patient and observant of colleagues who are acknowledged as models of exceptional teaching.

For example, Couros (n.d.) has suggested that the qualities that master teachers evidence include:

- Connecting with students first: For all students to excel, teachers must learn about them and connect with and attach to each child. This is not just about finding out how they learn, but it is finding out who they are. It is essential to know your students, learn their passions, and help them find out how we can engage them in their own learning.

- Teaching students first and curriculum second: Teachers must ensure that they differentiate learning and work to meet the needs of each student and understand how they each learn. Students have different learning styles and, as educators, it is vital to figure out how to help them meet their own needs so that they will excel in the subject areas taught.

- Ensuring that they draw relevance to curriculum: The question, "What does this have to do with real life?" is something that should not need to be said in a classroom. Not because it is not a legitimate question, but because teachers should understand the relevance of everything they teach. A master teacher knows that it is essential to use technology in the classroom to enhance learning in a way that is relevant to students.

- Working with students to develop a love of learning: Educators are obligated to teach curriculum objectives but we are also obligated professionally to help students find their own learning style. A master teacher will try to tap into those ways that students love to learn and build upon them. Creating that spark in each student will lead them to continued academic success and growth.

- Modeling and celebrating lifelong learning: A master teacher knows that she will never become the "perfect" teacher since that is unattainable. Master teachers will seek to grow along with their students. Education is a constantly evolving discipline and a master teacher knows that she needs to change with it to maintain relevance. Growth is essential as a teacher. Society changes continuously and so do its needs. The field of education needs reflective practitioners in the workplace and teachers must show that they are committed to such "habits of mind."

- Focusing on learning goals as opposed to performance goals: In the book *Drive*, Pink talks about the difference between performance and learning goals. A performance goal would be like having students desiring to receive an "A" in French; whereas, a learning goal would be represented in a student's desire to become fluent in the language. A master teacher sets goals based on learning not on simply receiving a grade.

- Ensuring that "character education" is an essential part of learning: Character education is just as relevant, if not more so, than any learning objectives set out in a curriculum. Collaboration is vital to success and working with others is an important skill. Working with students to teach the fundamentals of respecting others and being able to listen and learn from others is vital. Students can understand the learning objectives of a lesson, but not possess the ability to share these ideas with others in a respectful way. A master teacher ensures that students not only grow academically in class, but also socially and emotionally.

- Being passionate about the content they teach: If a teacher works in math and loves the subject area, that passion will spill over to the students he/she works with. A master teacher shares her passion and enthusiasm with her colleagues.

- A master teacher is a "school teacher:" It is essential that master teachers not only impact the learning environment of the class, but also have an impact on the school culture. This can happen in sharing their passion through extracurricular activities or their discrete skills with colleagues.

- Strong communication skills: Obviously, it is important that teachers can communicate with the students they teach, but what about their colleagues and parents? Sharing knowledge with colleagues is essential to the growth of the individual as well as the professional community. It is important that these skills are continuously developed and imperative that teachers effectively communicate with parents as they have insight about how their child learns best. A master teacher will effectively draw upon this knowledge.

Jackson (2012) similarly posits that some important characteristics of mastery teaching invariably includes: (a) start where your students are, (b) know where your students are going, (c) expect to get students to their goal, (d) support students along the way, (e) use feedback, (f) focus on quality, not quantity, and, interestingly, (g) never work harder than your students (n.p.).

Recently, Buskist, Sikorsky, Buckley, and Saville (2012) surveyed 916 undergraduates relative to the elements or qualities of master teaching and found the following ten to be perceived as the most representative (in order of importance): (a) realistic expectations/fair, (b) knowledgeable about topic, (c) understanding, (d) personable, (e) respectful, (f) creative/interesting, (g) positive/humorous, (h) encourages, cares for students, (i) flexible/openminded, (j) enthusiastic about teaching (p. 36).

The investigators simultaneously presented the same list of qualities to 118 faculty members and a comparison of the results showed that, whereas there was no hierarchical consensus among the two groups, the faculty participants included six of the students' top ten qualities in their ten most representative qualities list. Specifically, the faculty members valued: (a) knowledgeable about topic, (b) enthusiastic about teaching, (c) approachable/personable, (d) respectful, (e) creative/interesting, and (f) realistic expectations/fair, in that order. Clearly some of these qualities could be considered pedagogical skills and others appear to be associated with relationship-building.

Two Strategic Interventions Relevant to our Pedagogical Framework

The work of Redl (1966), which addresses behavioral and emotional crises in the school and classroom, can be quite helpful here, especially the elements of the "Life Space Interview" (LSI) that consists of both immediate "emotional first-aid-on-the-spot" as well as some "after action" teacher guidance. "The Life Space Interview" is a crisis intervention technique, developed for use by the classroom teacher, in which a student's behavior is discussed with her or him at the time of the problem's occurrence. There are two types of LSI. Both are "here and now" reactions to an event or experience in a student's life. The first, "Emotional-first-aid-on-the-spot," is used when the teacher wishes to help diffuse the problem quickly, and reintegrate the student back into the scheduled program. The "Clinical exploitation of life events" is a debriefing technique in which the teacher helps the student to gain insight into his or her behavior and change maladaptive responses to behavioral "triggers." There are five discrete interventions associated with the provision of "Emotional-first-aid-on-the-spot" described by Redl (1966) as:

- Drain Off Frustration Acidity: Allow the student to vent his/her emotions, but assist the individual in regaining control and calming down. (e.g., "I realize that it's your turn at bat, but we must go in now before the bell rings to signal the next class.").

- Support for the Management of Emotions: Help the student sort through events and put the problem in perspective.

- Communication Maintenance: Often, upon intervention, the student withdraws. Try to keep the student talking and communicating regardless of the topic of conversation.

- Regulation of Behavior and Social Traffic: This strategy involves the consistent application of rules and guidelines by a calm, patient adult.

- Umpire Services: The teacher makes a judgment in cases of inter-child and intra-child conflict after having reviewed all available information. A fair, impartial decision is presented and enforced.

The five elements of the "Clinical exploitation of life events," as described by Redl (1966) consist of the following:

- Reality Rub: The teacher helps the student to realize that she has misinterpreted or refused to recognize certain information pertinent to an incident.

- Value Repair and Restoration: The teacher attempts to awaken dormant values such as respect, empathy, trust, etc. The teacher attempts to "massage" the numb value areas and help develop appropriate emotional responses to certain situations.

- Symptom Estrangement: Some students don't realize that their behavior is inappropriate or bizarre in the eyes of others. The teacher brings the student's attention to the specific behavior and how it is viewed by others.

- New Tool Salesmanship: In this interview, the student is helped to improve his ability to react in a problem-solving situation. "Tools" or ways of solving problems are taken from experience and applied in new situations.

- Manipulation of the Boundaries of the Self: This interview is used with two types of students: those who allow themselves to be "used" by others, and those who victimize or take advantage of others.

The process of implementation of any of the "Life Space Interviewing" techniques involves, (1) intervening; (2) listening to all parties involved in a nonjudgmental manner; (3) analyzing the situation to determine whether the behavior is acute (an atypical or episodic occurrence) or chronic (frequently recurring); (4) select a specific LSI approach; (5) implement the approach or approaches in a respectful, attentive, and professional manner, and finally, (6) combine or modify the relevant approach or approaches as required by the circumstance.

Three other simple, evidenced-based interventions that might prove helpful to teachers working with students who display challenging behaviors are:

- Behavior-specific praise: predicated on four principles; namely, that the praise must be immediate, it must also be specific and must include details that describe the acknowledged prosocial behavior, it must be offered contingent, exclusively, on the presentation of the desired behavior, and it must be frequent (Conroy, Sutherland, Snyder, Al-Hendawi, & Vo, 2009).

- Behavior momentum: involves the following four steps: (a) identify problem tasks (those that are most onerous to the student), (b) identify easy tasks (those the student is likely to complete because they are easily performed), (c) collect data to validate both the "problem" and "easy" tasks, and (d) implement the intervention by first asking the student to complete "easy" tasks, with a high probability of complicity, then introduce a "problem" task (one with a lower probability of completion). Research suggests that by introducing a student to "easy" tasks first, there is a greater likelihood that the student will be more predisposed to completing the "problem" or hard task (Lee, Balfiore, & Budin, 2008).

- Implementing choice: a behavioral approach that consists of the following four stages: (a) identify problem activities or contexts, (b) identify choices that might be afforded in each context, (c) implement "choice" in one context at a time, and (d) if effective, implement the "choice" in different contexts or circumstances.

For example, a student might be provided options or choices relative to the order of assignment completion, the type of assignment (portfolio, essay, report), where to work on the assigned task (classroom, library, outdoors, at a desk, table, or on the floor), and the type of reward or reinforcement the student can earn upon successful completion of the assignment that are desirable to the student and reasonable to the teacher. Finally, of course, the "choice" must produce measurable benefit relative to the student's behavior (Kern & Parks, 2012; Kern & State, 2009). [excerpted from Landrum & Sweigart, 2014].

Conclusion

The investigation of effective teaching and sound pedagogy has revealed that the essence of good teaching is, at its best, an amalgam of an art, a science, and a craft. The term "pedagogy" can be simply and effectively defined as: "any conscious activity by one person designed to enhance the learning of another" (Watkins & Mortimore, 1999). Alexander (2004) expands on this definition of pedagogy by adding that, to be considered useful and effective, it must provide students with what they need to know, it must evidence the skills needed to impart that knowledge, and it must demonstrate the commitment necessary to make the daily decisions about instruction and learning required of an effective teacher (p. 11).

Good teachers take the time to really know themselves, strive to be honest with themselves about who they are and what they know and believe, and be courageous in that revelation; for example, in the pursuit of the "identity" and "integrity" of the teacher (Palmer, 1997; Loughran, 2002). Similarly, researchers (Austin et al., 2011; Korthagen, 2004) propose the authenticity of self as a tenet of effective teacher pedagogy. As Loughran (2002) affirms, "why" we teach affects "how" we teach.

In addition to these pedagogical characteristics, Russell (1997), Schon (1983), and Sellars (2013) encourage "self-reflection" as another important aspect of sound pedagogy while Noddings (2005) and Smith (2012) extol the importance of developing caring teacher-student relationships as vital to any notion of pedagogy. Freire (1970) and Bruner (1996) stress the importance of understanding the teacher's culture and its relevance to the classroom, as well as the cultural milieu of her students.

Nonetheless, a pedagogical framework was inspired by the work of Ireson, Mortimore, and Hallam (1999) that identified six critical elements. The first of these is the requirement that such a pedagogical schema be clearly understood and operationally defined. Second, the author's framework cannot consist of faddish techniques - it is not a toolbox of instructional strategies, rather it should offer teachers a theoretical foundation upon which to build a contextually and culturally viable pedagogy. Third, a viable pedagogical framework is predicated on the value of teachers - they need to see their worth to their students, their profession, and their society. Educators need to develop their identities as professionals and ultimately must, as Stout (2005) exhorts, cultivate "certainty, positivity, and the unity of self and moral goals" (p. 194). Accordingly, [teachers] should be able to say, without reservation, "who I am is what I want to do and what I am doing" (Stout, 2005, p. 195). In other words, teachers should be persons of or in pursuit of integrity.

As the elements continue, the fourth, context matters in the development of a sound pedagogical framework. Specifically, teachers must be able to impart an understanding of social cues and an understanding of the value of cultural nuance as well as the "hidden curriculums" of our social structures. Fifth, a sound pedagogy must empower students to identify their strengths and weaknesses, and take responsibility for their own learning. Teachers that possess such a pedagogical foundation should motivate and entice learners, help them to learn how to be with others, how to love, take criticism, grieve, and have fun as well as how to add, subtract, multiply, and divide (Tompkins, 1996, p. xvi). Lastly, this pedagogical framework acknowledges and celebrates the notion that teachers are learners too and to be relevant and effective, they must cultivate a love of learning and bring their passion for learning into the classroom every day.

A final recommendation as it relates to the development of a pedagogical framework. Smith (2012) suggests three elements considered as vital to a sound pedagogy; namely, "animation," "reflection," and "action." By "animation," he is referring to "bringing life into situations and introducing students to new experiences." He describes "reflection" as "creating moments and spaces to explore lived experiences." Lastly, he defines "action" to mean "working with people so that they are able to make changes in their lives" (p. 10). This suggested "pedagogical framework" provides a useful schema for teachers to further develop into educators that are contextually viable for their specific teaching experiences and needs.

Points to Remember

- *The proliferation of inclusion and Response to Intervention requires that all teachers, both special and general educators, be adequately prepared to successfully teach students with and without disabilities.*

- *The profession of "teaching" is best understood as an amalgam of science and art; truly a "craft" (Gage, 1978) that can best be achieved through the "identity" and "integrity" of the educator (Palmer, 1998; Stout, 2005).*

- *The three "tenets" of successful teaching include: (a) positive student-teacher relationships, (b) effective pedagogical skills, and (c) subject knowledge (and a "passion" for what one teaches).*

- *"Attachment Theory" is most relevant to the development of a sound pedagogy because it requires that the teacher examine the dynamic effects of her parental and cultural influences on the way she views her students and their "challenging" behaviors.*

- *The value of "self-reflection" or the ability to think critically about the effects of one's teaching on the emotional, behavioral, and intellectual development of one's students, is an important aspect of sound pedagogy (Russell, 1997; Schon, 1983; Sellars, 2013).*

- *The three elements critical to a viable pedagogy include: animation (introducing student to new experiences), reflection (creating moments and spaces to explore lived experiences), and action (working with student so that they are able to make changes in their lives) (Smith, 2012).*

References

Alexander, R. (2004). *Still no pedagogy? Principle, pragmatism and compliance in primary education.* Cambridge, UK: University of Cambridge.

Austin, V., Barowsky, E., Malow, M., & Gomez, D. (2011). Effective teacher behaviors evident in successful teachers of students with emotional and behavioral disorders. *Journal of the American Academy of Special Education Professionals.* Retrieved from https://eric.ed.gov/?id=EJ1136998

Bolles, R. N. (2015). *What color is your parachute? A practical manual for job-hunters and career-changers.* New York, NY: Ten Speed Press.

Bowlby, J. (1958). The nature of the child's tie to his mother. *The International Journal of Psychoanalysis,* 39, 350–373. Retrieved from https://www.ncbi.nlm.nih.gov/pubmed/13610508

Bruner, J. (1996). *The Culture of Education.* Boston: Harvard University Press.

Buskist, W., Sikorski, J., Buckley, T., & Saville, B. K. (2002). Elements of master teaching. In S. F. Davis & W. Buskist (Eds.), *The teaching of psychology: Essays in honor of Wilbert J. McKeachie and Charles L. Brewer* (pp. 27–39). Mahwah, NJ: Lawrence Erlbaum. Cambridge Dictionary Online (2012). *Pedagogy.* http://dictionary.cambridge.org/us/.

Cavin, C. (1998). Maintaining Sanity in an Insane Classroom: How a Teacher of Students with Emotional Disturbances Can Keep from Becoming an Emotionally Disturbed Teacher. *Education and Treatment of Children,* 21(3), 370-84. Retrieved from https://eric.ed.gov/?id=EJ581781

Cogill, J. (2008). *Primary teachers' interactive whiteboard practice across one year: Changes in pedagogy and influencing factors.* Ed.D. thesis, King's College, University of London.

Conroy, M. A., Sutherland, K. S., Snyder, A., Al-Hendawi, M., & Vo, A. (2009). Creating a positive classroom atmosphere: Teachers' use of effective praise and feedback. *Beyond Behavior,* 18(2), 18–26. Retrieved from https://eric.ed.gov/?id=EJ869681

Corbett, J. & Norwich, B. (1999). Learners with special educational needs. In P. Mortimore (Ed.), *Understanding pedagogy and its impact on learning* (pp. 115–136). London, UK: Paul Chapman Publishing.

Couros, G. (n.d.). *What makes a master teacher? The principal of change: Stories of learning and leading.* Retrieved from http://georgecouros.ca/blog/archives/267.

Freire, P. (1970). *Pedagogy of the oppressed.* New York, NY: Herder and Herder.

Gage, N. L. (1978). *The scientific basis of the art of teaching.* New York, NY: Teachers College Press.

Gundem, B. B. (December 07, 1992). Vivat Comenius: A Commemorative Essay on Johann Amos Comenius, 1592-1670. *Journal of Curriculum and Supervision,* 8, 1, 43-55. Retrieved from https://eric.ed.gov/?id=EJ452789

Hjalmarsson, R. (2008). Criminal justice involvement and high school completion.

Journal of Urban Economics, 63(2), 613-630. Retrieved from Retrieved from www.sciencedirect.com/science/article/pii/S0094119007000642

Ireson, J., Mortimore, P. & Hallahan, S. (1999). The common strands of pedagogy and their

implications. In P. Mortimore (ed.) *Understanding Pedagogy and its Impact on Learning.* London, UK: Paul Chapman, Publishers.

Jackson, R. R. (2012). *Never work harder than your students & other principles of great teaching.* Alexandria, VA: Association for Supervision and Curriculum Development.

Korthagen, F. A. J. (2004). In search of the essence of a good teacher: Towards a more holistic approach in teacher education. *Teaching and Teacher Education,* 20, 7797. Retrieved from www.sciencedirect.com/science/article/pii/S0742051X03001185

Landrum, T. J. & Sweigart, C. A. (2014). *Simple, evidence-based interventions for classic problems of emotional and behavioral disorders. Beyond Behavior,* 23(3), 3–8. DOI:10.1177/107429561402300302

Lee, D. L., Belfiore, P. J., & Budin, S. G. (2008). Creating a momentum of school success. *Teaching Exceptional Children,* 40(3), 65–70. DOI:10.1177/004005990804000307

Loughran, J. J. (2002). Effective reflective practice: In search of meaning in learning about teaching. *Journal of Teacher Education,* 53(1), 33-43. DOI: 10.1177/0022487102053001004

Mascolo, M. F. (2009). Beyond student-centered and teacher-centered pedagogy: Teaching and learning as guided participation. *Pedagogy and the Human Sciences,* 1(1), 3-27.

Mendel, R. A. (2011). No Place for Kids: The Case for Reducing Juvenile Incarceration. Annie E. Casey Foundation. Retrieved from http://www.aecf.org/m/resourcedoc/aecf-NoPlaceForKidsFullReport-2011.pdf

Noddings, N. (2005). *The Challenge to Care in Schools.* New York: Teachers College Press.

Northfield, J., & Gunstone, R. (1997). Teacher Education as a process of developing teacher

knowledge. In *Teaching about teaching: purpose, passion and pedagogy in teacher education* (pp. 48 - 56). London, UK: Falmer.

Palmer, P. J. (1998). *The courage to teach.* San Francisco: Jossey-Bass.

Redl, F. (1966). *The life-space interview: Strategy and techniques. When we deal with children.* New York, NY: Free Press.

Russell, T. (1997). Teaching teachers: How I teach IS the message. In J. Loughran & T. Russell (Eds.), *Teaching about teaching: Purpose, passion and pedagogy in teacher education* (pp. 32-47). London, England: Falmer.

Schon, D. (1983). *The reflective practitioner: How professionals think in action.* New York, NY: Basic Books.

Sellars, M. (2013). *Reflective practice for teachers.* London, England: Sage.

Smith, M. (2012). Social pedagogy from a Scottish perspective. *International Journal of Social Pedagogy,* 1(1), 46–55. Retrieved from thempra.org.uk/ojs_files/journals/1/articles/3/public/3-32-1-PB.pdf

U.S. Department of Education, Office of Special Education and Rehabilitative Services, Office of Special Education Programs, 28th Annual Report to Congress on the Implementation of the *Individuals with Disabilities Education Act, 2006,* vol. 1, Washington, D.C., 2009.

Vygotsky, L. S. (1987). *The collected works of L.S. Vygotsky: Vol. I: Problems of general psychology.* R. Rieber & A. Carton (Eds.), N. Minick (Trans.). New York, NY: Plenum Press. (Original work published 1934).

Watkins, C. & Mortimer, P. (1999). Pedagogy: What do we know? In Mortimer P (Ed) (1999). *Understanding pedagogy and its impact on teaching.* (pp 1-19) London, England: Chapman.

Chapter 7

Parents Make the Difference: Fostering Emotional Resiliency to Improve School Outcomes

Elizabeth Jean, *Endicott College*
and Nicholas D. Young, *American International College*

Parents play an important role in making school a positive experience for children. This is especially true for students with learning disabilities who tend to get more easily frustrated. By understanding what emotional resiliency is parents can be the role model and provide the necessary stepping stones to help their children. While emotional resilience is inborn, it is also taught, and knowing what and how to teach these skills makes all the difference.

Emotional resiliency is the ability to handle stressful situations and the optimism to continue when things get difficult (Lechner, 2017; Scott, 2017). It has also been defined as the ability to adapt to adversity, trauma, threats or stress, to "spring back" after an emotionally difficult time (South Lakes Federation, 2014, p. 9). South Lakes Federation (2014) also states that emotional resilience has three related parts: (1) Self-esteem/confidence, (2) self-efficacy and the ability to adapt to situations, and (3) a collection of problem-solving techniques for social settings.

Emotional resilience is based on protective factors that are attributes of individuals and/or families that "reduce risk and promote well-being of children and families" (Children's Bureau, 2016, n.p.). There are six protective factors including nurturing and attachment, parental resilience, social connections, concrete support in times of need, knowledge of child development and parenting skills, and social and emotional competence (Center for the Study of Social Policy, 2017). In total, these protective factors increase resiliency and lead to student success over the long run.

Dissecting resiliency even deeper, there are seven separate factors that lead to resilient children (Ginsburg, 2015). Once the parents of children with learning disabilities use these strengths to their advantage, their children will be more able to adapt in the face of challenging work and school issues (American Psychological Association, 2017). It is incumbent on the parent to take steps of their own to ensure a strong bond between home and school as a way to make the educational process work for their child.

The Seven Factors of Resiliency

There is no doubt that stress plays a role in the day to day life of students – especially that of a student with a learning disability. They must learn to adapt, to tweak their thinking, to learn new ways of thinking about a problem, and to constantly remind themselves that they can do the work. The way in which this student handles the situation is due in part to innate factors but also a series of learned behaviors that help them "negotiate their own challenges" (American Academy of Pediatrics, 2015, p. 2).

The seven protective factors of families that lead to resilient children, according to Ginsburg (2015) are used as guidelines for parents who wish to build inner strength and abilities in their children. These are especially important for students with learning disabilities who often feel frustrated by their perceived lack of ability and frustration with the work at hand. The seven factors include: character, competence, confidence, connection, contribution, control, and coping (Ginsburg, 2015). Each aspect of resiliency contributes to the student feeling an overall sense of well-being and ability (American Academy of Pediatrics, 2015):

- Character: Parents must guide their children to have morals and values that provide a strong sense of right and wrong. Ensure a safe place to talk and an ability to have open dialog. Additionally, it is important to help children form healthy relationships with both children and adults.

- Competence: A child who believes he or she can handle a situation has achieved competence. Parents should focus on student strengths while identifying and working on perceived weaknesses. It is also imperative to empower students, especially those with learning disabilities, to make decisions – right or wrong – they will learn from both.

- Confidence: A student achieves confidence through competence or a belief in personal ability. It is vital that parents use authentic praise and focus on the positive. By focusing on the best qualities a student exhibits, he begins to see himself as competent and exudes confidence.

- Connection: Creating opportunities to bring family and community together is important for building a sense of security. Children need to feel that they are safe to express their emotions and where nurturing healthy relationships emphasizes a message of positivity.

- Contribution: Students need to understand that their contributions to the world are significant. Parents can reinforce this concept through serving others in the home such as a grandparent or another student with a disability or in the community, such as a soup kitchen or donating gently used clothes and toys.

- Control: Students who realize they have control over the outcome of a particular situation are better able to move from situation to situation. Empowering students to make good choices and use positive actions move them in the proper direction. Additionally, parents who are able to use discipline as a method to teach, not punish, will find their children understand the connection between action and consequence.

- Coping: While last on the list, coping skills are the conduit that help students overcome challenges and move towards success. Modeling appropriate skills help children understand that all human beings find some situations challenging but that there are ways to handle situations that do not involve risk-taking or negativity.

Several well-known groups have written about the need for resiliency in children/students (American Academy of Pediatrics, 2015; American Psychological Association, 2017; Education Week, 2017). The parent is the first adult responsible for creating emotional resiliency in their children, especially those with learning disabilities, which in turn gives these students a platform for success. Parents should also make strong connections with the school as a secondary measure of creating resiliency and well-being for the student with learning disabilities.

Strategies for Parents to Improve School Outcomes

It is important to remember that "resiliency refers to achieving positive outcomes despite challenges or threatening circumstances"

(Lechner, 2017; Zolkoski & Bullock, 2012). Study after study shows the importance of resiliency as a means to increasing student outcomes (Zolkoski & Bullock, 2012; Topor, Keane, Shelton, & Calkins, 2010; Garrett, 2014). This happens first through parent interactions with the child, especially in their early years. Once the child enters school, however, the parent must also make solid connections with the school. Engaging the leadership and academic team using strategies that will help increase student resiliency is a must, especially for students with disabilities.

While a plethora of strategies exist, they can be broken down into several broad categories including engagement, organization, parent as advocate, parent volunteerism, organization, and growth mindset (Dweck, 2017). Each one offers parents a chance to work with the school team directly responsible for their child. These connections lead to a better environment for the student with a learning disability; not only is the parent actively working with the school/educator but the student sees the importance of the connection between home and school.

Engagement

The first federal mandate to offer equal access to education was the Elementary and Secondary Education Act (ESEA); signed into law in 1965. Ten years later the Individuals with Disabilities Education Act (IDEA) of 1975, followed by No Child Left Behind (NCLB) of 2002, and most recently Every Student Succeeds Act (ESSA) of 2015, have each built on the previous iteration to ensure access and educational support to students and families.

As part of ESSA, schools are tasked to reach out to families to bridge the gap that often exists between home and school (U.S. Department of Education, 2015). Providing monies and guidelines, schools are instructed to not only involve parents in the special education process, but also partner with families to provide a continuum of service and take active roles in the decision-making process (Duncan, 2016; Henderson, 2016).

This expanded definition of home school partnership also suggests that parents play a significant role guiding their child successfully through a complex educational system as well as being an active advocate for a public school experience that is both shared and effective (Epstein, 2011; Mapp & Kuttner, 2013). Grant and Ray (2015) explain that family engagement requires "a mutually collaborative, working relationship with the family [that] serves the best interests of the student, in both school and home settings, for the primary purpose of increasing student achievement" (p. 6).

Engagement is often defined as the act of coming together; taking part in something; doing with as opposed to doing to (Merriam-Webster, 2017). Using this definition, it is easy to see how parents who take an active part in their child's education will teach resiliency through modeling. Engaging with educational staff to provide the necessary components for a student with learning disabilities is equally important as staff making such a connection.

Parents should reach out to the educator, school counselor, and service providers (American Psychological Association, 2015). It is important to have regular meetings where collaboration and communication are present so that the discussion surrounds student progress, what the parent can do at home, as well as next steps. If the student is too young to be included in the meeting, the parent should make sure to have conversations with the student in advance as well as after the meeting takes place. Asking questions such as "How are you feeling about school?" "What is most difficult for you?" and "What do you see as your strengths?" help the parent share information about the child as well as receive feedback at the meeting vital to the success of the student.

Families who engage with educators and the staff that provide academic and other services to the student with learning disabilities provide a visual model of resiliency that the student can emulate as he or she matures in school. This partnership approach to education ensures that everyone is on the same page, working towards similar goals, using collaboration and communication as essential components to adapt and manage situations that may be stressful (American Psychological Association, 2015). Similar to engagement, the parent as an advocate for the student with learning disabilities is another tool available to model resiliency and achieve well-being.

Parent as Advocate

The parent has intimate knowledge about the child with a learning disability; after all, he or she has spent many years with this youngster. Although the parent may not know educational specifics, it is important to advocate for best practice and developmentally appropriate education. Several pundits (Gurland, 2016; Scholastic, 2017) offer a checklist of items that assist the parent in being a proactive advocate as a way to increase student resiliency. The list includes making contact with the teacher, building a relationship with the school, keeping records, knowing your power, learning your rights, knowing that you are not alone (Gurland, 2016; Scholastic, 2017).

- Make contact with the teacher: It is important to remember that the first line of defense is usually the teacher of record. This educator most likely works directly with the student on a daily basis and can give firsthand information as to how the student is doing, as well as what the family can do to assist.

- Build a relationship with the school: Having a child with a learning disability means a long-term collaboration with the school. It is vital that the parent begins by learning about the school and district, understanding what services are available and, most importantly, how to go about making a partnership that puts the student first.

- Keep records: The parent who keeps records has clear documentation of what has been said and how the IEP or 504 has been implemented. It is important to document conversations, keep copies of IEPs, 504s, and progress notes. When a concern exists, put it in writing and send it to all parties that may be involved.

- Know your power: The parent is the best advocate – he or she comes from a place of intimate knowledge and passion regarding the student. It is imperative that the parent be confident, bringing student strengths and weaknesses to the table.

- Learn your rights: The goal of education is to prepare students for post-secondary education or employment and at a most basic level to live independently. Parents should review IDEA (1965) and ESSA (2015) so that the basics are understood. It is always best to try and work with staff to find solutions; however, when conflict arises, know that mediation is an option that listens to both sides and takes a non-biased view on the issue at hand.

- Know that you are not alone: Parents need to connect with others through parent-teacher organizations, school groups, district, state or federally funded resource centers. This reminds them that they are not alone and that others share or understand what they are going through. Many of

Parents Make the Difference 113

these groups offer conferences and workshops regarding the IEP process, student and parent rights, parenting classes, and more.

Stay Involved/Volunteer

While being involved and volunteering is also part of the parent as advocate list, it is important to understand the significance in terms of connecting home and school and emotional resilience. Two-way communication may help both parties understand the school day and home life of a student with a learning disability (Epstein, 2011). Likewise, a parent who volunteers in class with academics, simple preparation tasks or even on field trips begins to understand more about student life and resiliency (Scholastic, 2017).

Staying involved with the school may be as simple as a communication log sent back and forth each day between parent and educator/service provider. While the educator may see this as time-consuming and an uncomfortable task, it gives the parent good information about how the student is doing and what he or she can do at home to help (Mapp & Kuttner, 2013). Likewise, if the student with a learning disability has had a tough morning or has expressed a concern at home, the parent can address it easily to the educator who can then take this into consideration during the day (Gurland, 2016).

Volunteering in the classroom gives the parent a glimpse into classroom rules, rituals, protocols, and expectations; however, parents must respect the classroom dynamics and follow the directions of the educator (Project Appleseed, 2017). This insider's view allows the parent to better understand the student's day and offers the parent the chance to give emotional support at home; thus, furthering resiliency (Project Appleseed, 2017; Scholastic, 2017a). Perhaps the student finds a particular subject more difficult; the parent who is able to watch the educator might learn a trick as to how best help the student (Bantuveris, 2013).

Organization

A student with learning disabilities who is disorganized faces unneeded stress and may not be as resilient as possible. During meetings and conferences the parent can ask for accommodations or modifications to be made to assignments, easing the homework expectations. At home, it is important for the parent to use a predictable routine/schedule and limit distractions with a regular workspace when completing homework, as both will eliminate stress (Dawson, 2010; Parent to Parent of Georgia, n.d.).

As a stress reduction tool, and thus a resiliency strategy, providing a clutter-free area for homework shows the student the importance of academic practice (Parent to Parent of Georgia, n.d.). Knowing that the student may struggle with the work and the workload, the parent may wish to provide a specific time frame in which to complete the work, including breaks and a snack (Dawson, 2010). These strategies reinforce the importance of education and school goals while acknowledging the struggle.

Growth Mindset

Growth mindset can be described as the belief that basic abilities can be developed through hard work and dedication (Dweck, 2017). This positive attitude, when seen in parents by children with learning disabilities, creates resiliency. Ways for parents to increase growth mindset include celebrating mistakes, praising the process not the person, and reminding children to never give up (Lechner, 2017; Dweck, 2017). Parental positivity and a growth mindset create "a love of learning and a resilience that is essential for great accomplishment" (Dweck, 2017); thus, students with learning disabilities who are exposed to these are more likely to have improved school outcomes.

Parents who exhibit mindfulness traits are those who consistently use positive word choices, surround themselves with other positive and like-minded people, adopt a flexible thinking pattern, set goals that align with a specific purpose and reflect daily (Lechner, 2017). Students with learning disabilities can emulate these traits with the help of their families as another strategy that leads to emotional resiliency.

Conclusion

Fostering emotional resiliency, or having optimism in the face of adversity, in children with learning disabilities is more easily accomplished by the parent who is committed to the good fight. Protective factors can reduce risk and increase well-being and are the first line of defense for families (Ginsburg, 2015). Beyond protective factors, there are strategies that parents can implement to increase resiliency and improve school outcomes.

Broad categories of parental strategies exist that can make significant improvements in students and outcomes. These include engagement and partnership with schools and educators, parents who advocate in positive ways for their students, and volunteering in the school and classroom of the student. Additionally, it is important for families to organize the home to improve homework outcomes and use a growth mindset. Collectively, these strategies ensure that students with learning disabilities can become resilient students who are capable of accomplishing great things and improving academic outcomes.

Points to Remember

- *Emotional resiliency is the ability to handle stressful situations and rebound with some degree of ease.*

- *Protective factors are parental attributes that lead to student well-being by reducing risk. They include: nurturing and attachment, parental resilience, social connections, support in times of need, knowledge of child development and parenting skills, and social and emotional competence.*

- *Parental strategies for creating resilience in students with learning disabilities include: engaging with schools in deep and meaningful partnerships, advocating for successful student outcomes, volunteering within the classroom, having an organizational method at home that supports learning.*

- *Growth mindset is perhaps the most important strategy as it can be developed over time with determination and hard work. Parents need to praise the process not the person, celebrate the mistakes and work through possible solutions, as well as reminding the child not to give up.*

- *Mindfulness, as part of the growth mindset, leads to resilience. Parents who use positive word choice, have flexible thinking patterns, set goals, surround themselves with like-minded people and reflect daily are able to set the example for their children.*

References

American Academy of Pediatrics. (2015). Building resilience in children. Retrieved from http://www.apa.org/helpcenter/resilience.aspx

American Psychological Association. (2017). 10 tips for building resilience in children and teens. Retrieved from http://www.apa.org/helpcenter/resilience.aspx

Bantuveris, K. (2013). 5 tips for engaging parent volunteers in the classroom. Retrieved from https://www.edutopia.org/blog/strategies-for-engaging-parent-volunteers-karen-bantuveris

Center for the Study of Social Policy. (2017). Protective capacities and protective factors. Retrieved from https://www.cssp.org/reform/strengtheningfamilies/about/body/ProtectiveFactorsActionSheets.pdf

Children's Bureau. (2017). Protective factors to promote well-being. Retrieved from https://www.childwelfare.gov/topics/preventing/promoting/protectfactors/

Dawson, P. (2010). Homework: A guide for parents. Retrieved from https://webcache.googleusercontent.com/search?q=cache:DH2Wp086rqwJ:https://www.nasponline.org/Documents/Resources%2520and%2520Publications/Handouts/Families%2520and%2520Educators/Homework_a_Guide_for_Parents.pdf+&cd=1&hl=en&ct=clnk&gl=us

Duncan, A. (2015). ESEA Speech to Congress. Retrieved from http://www.ed.gov/blog/2015/01/opportunity-is-not-optional-secretary-duncans-vision-for-americas-landmark-education-law/

Dweck, C.S. (2017). Mindset. Retrieved from https://www.gvsu.edu/ftlc/mindset-carol-dweck-183.htm

Epstein, J. L. (2011). School, family, and community partnerships: Preparing educators and improving schools (2nd ed.). Boulder, CO: Westview Press.

Garrett, M. (2014). Play-based interventions and resilience in children. Retrieved from http://www.academicjournals.org/journal/IJPC/article-full-text-pdf/6B0031748863

Ginsburg, K. (2015). A parent's guide to building resilience in children and teens: Giving your child roots and wings. Elk Grove Village, IL: American Academy of Pediatrics.

Grant, K. B., & Ray, J. A. (2015). Home, school, and community collaboration: Culturally responsive family engagement (3rd ed.). Thousand Oaks, CA: Sage Publications, Inc.

Gurland, G. (2016). How to advocate successfully for your child: What every parent should know about special education. Charleston, S.C.: Create Space Independent Publishing Platform.

Henderson, A.T. (2016). Quick brief on family engagement in Every Child Succeeds Act (ESSA) of 2015. Retrieved from https://ra.nea.org/wp-content/uploads/2016/06/FCE-in-ESSA-in-Brief.pdf

Lechner, T. (2017). Resilience and Grit: How to develop a growth mindset. Retrieved from http://www.chopra.com/articles/resilience-and-grit-how-to-develop-a-growth-mindset#sm.000012epmat1h3d24wytq7ocgbtkx

Mapp, K. L., Kuttner, P. J. (2013). Partners in education: A dual capacity-building framework for family-school partnerships. Retrieved from http://www.ed.gov/parent-and-family-engagementMassachusetts Department of Education.

Matthiessen. C. (2015). Is your child resilient? Retrieved from https://www.greatschools.org/gk/articles/is-your-child-resilient/

Merriam-Webster. (2017). Engage. Retrieved from https://www.merriam-webster.com/dictionary/engage

Parent to Parent of Georgia. (n.d.). Helping your child with disabilities with homework. Retrieved from https://www.gadoe.org/Curriculum-Instruction-and-Assessment/Special-Education-Services/Documents/Parent%20Fact%20Sheets/Helping%20your%20Child%20with%20Disabilities%20with%20Homework%2010-12.pdf

Project Appleseed. (2017). Benefits & barriers to family involvement in education. Retrieved from http://www.projectappleseed.org/barriers

Scholastic. (2017). Be your child's advocate. Retrieved from http://www.scholastic.com/parents/resources/article/parent-teacher-partnerships/be-your-childs-advocate

Scholastic. (2017a). Volunteering in the classroom. Retrieved from http://www.scholastic.com/parents/resources/article/volunteering-fundraising/volunteering-classroom

Scott, E. (2017). The traits, benefits and development of emotional resilience. Retrieved from https://www.verywell.com/emotional-resilience-is-a-trait-you-can-develop-3145235

South Lakes Federation. (2014). Emotional Resilience: Useful resources for schools. Retrieved from https://positivepsychologyprogram.com/wp-content/uploads/2017/06/Emotional-resilience-.pdf

Topor, D.R., Keane, S.P., Shelton, T.L., & Calkins, S.D. (2010). Parent involvement and student academic performance: A multiple mediational analysis. Retrieved from https://www.ncbi.nlm.nih.gov/pmc/articles/PMC3020099/

U.S. Department of Education. (2015). Every Student Succeeds Act. Retrieved from https://www.ed.gov/essa?src=rn

Zolkoski, S.M. & Bullock, L.M. (2012). Resilience in children and youth: A review. Retrieved from file:///C:/Users/Elizabeth/Downloads/Resilience%20in%20children%20and%20youth-A%20review.pdf

Chapter 8

Working with Students Who Have Experienced Trauma: Educating Teachers About Trauma-Informed Practice

Micheline Malow, *Manhattanville College*

Teachers are tasked with managing an array of social-emotional and behavioral difficulties in the classroom; most of which they feel unprepared for. In an effort to understand the varied difficulties children bring to school, teachers sometimes label them as disengaged, unmotivated, inattentive, and/or disruptive. With those labels as a starting point, teachers then seek to remediate the problem with classroom management strategies they have been taught in their teacher preparation programs. These behaviorally based strategies call for planned ignoring of inappropriate behaviors, cueing and prompting students to engage suitably, and positively reinforcing the suitable behaviors once displayed. When looking into the origin of classroom behaviors, however, teachers may be surprised to discover that childhood experiences of trauma frequently manifest themselves as social-emotional and/or behavioral difficulties (Sitler, 2008). With this in mind, teachers need to explore whether the observed learning and emotional-behavioral difficulties in the classroom have neurodevelopmental or trauma origins.

Determining the origin of the difficulty is necessary in order to facilitate healing in the children and supporting the children in recovery from trauma will allow the secondary difficulties to remit naturally. All children in the classroom, those with and without trauma histories, have similar needs from their teachers – to be seen as a whole, unique, individual who requires care and attention in order for learning to advance.

Defining Trauma

Although compassionate individuals wish the best for one another, circumstances beyond control, as well as difficulties encountered during daily living, increase the odds that negative experiences will occur. The exposure to these experiences is often internalized as personal trauma. Trauma in and of itself is not an event; however, the way an individual reflects on the experience can elicit an automatic stressful response. Nevertheless, trauma is different than ordinary life stressors. An event or situation is potentially traumatizing if it is unpredictable or uncontrollable by the person experiencing it. Given that a child's response to an event is individual, potentially traumatizing events (PTE), as termed by researchers Litz, Miller, Ruef, and McTeeague, (2002), cause a sense of fear, terror and helplessness.

Potentially traumatizing events include events that may manifest as physical injury, sexual assault, the observation of violence or suffering, as well as the experience of extreme poverty. With such a range of experiences that may result in the experience of trauma, PTEs are acknowledged as widespread and are unfortunately experienced by approximately 48 percent (almost 35 million) of children in the United States (Bartlett, Smith, & Bringewatt, 2017). While the 48 percent estimate seems high, the American Psychological Association estimate is higher, stating that more than two-thirds of children under the age of 16 have experienced a traumatizing event (APA, 2008).

As noted, PTEs are not singular experiences and are thus not understood by each child in the same way. Some traumatic incidents can occur as acute, one-time events and impact the child in the short-term (Deihl, 2013; Wright, 2014). Natural disasters, accidents, and tragic human events such as school shootings, fall into this category. Conversely, traumatic experiences can be chronic with repeated exposure to the PTE encompassing a way of life for the child (Deihl, 2013; Wright, 2014). Events in this category of trauma include child maltreatment, domestic abuse, chronic illness, extreme poverty, and exposure to neighborhood violence. Whether the PTE is an acute or chronic experience, in the time frame immediately following the event nearly all children will manifest distress of some sort.

Although unfortunate, some children will be exposed to multiple sources of trauma. This situation is known as complex trauma. Complex trauma depicts a chronic, developmental situation that reflects exposure to multiple sources of trauma and ongoing exposure that complicates the child's ability to understand and successfully process the situation (O'Neill, Guenette, & Kitchenham, 2010; Purvis, Cross, Dansereau, & Parris, 2013). As the PTEs are experienced over time, the child's development is impacted, although the specific areas of difficulty and ability to recover are dependent on multiple factors. Ultimately, factors such as the age of the child, whether the trauma is acute or chronic, and the presence of ecological risk and protective characteristics determine the child's ability to recover (Bartlett, et al., 2017).

Theoretical Understanding of Trauma

Awareness of the complexity of trauma has propelled researchers to not only define what PTEs and trauma are but to also understand how and why children experience trauma as they do. The origins of trauma can be understood best by utilizing the theoretical perspective of Uri Bronfenbrenner's Ecological Systems Theory (Bronfenbrenner, 1986). Bronfenbrenner states that each child develops as a result of bi-directional influences exerted from proximal and distal forces. Although the child's unique biological and psychological characteristics sit at the center of Bronfenbrenner's model, situational forces exerted from systems that radiate out from the child-centered model, such as the family, school, community, and the larger cultural context within which the child exists, also impact the child's developmental trajectory. Working from this perspective, the child does not exist in isolation; there are multiple sources of risk and support that wield influence, just as the child influences the other systems.

In an attempt to understand PTEs, identifying areas of risk and support within the child's proximal and distal systems becomes an important step on the child's road to recovery. The child's personal characteristics, family, friends, and school personnel are all proximal influences that can help or hinder recovery; just as the more distal influences of school policies, state agencies, and legal requirements can also help or hinder recovery from complex developmental trauma.

The relational well-being of the child is impacted during PTEs (Bartlett, et al., 2017; Day, Somers, Baroni, West, Sanders, & Peterson, 2015; Wright, 2014). Trauma impacts not only the way children view themselves, but it also changes how children relate to other peers and adults in their world. "If a child thinks that the world is out to get him or that his guardians are unable to keep him safe, growing up becomes very scary indeed" (Wright, 2014, p. 89). Attachment Theory (Bowlby, 1969) details children's need to form and maintain secure attachments. Bowlby advanced that relationships established early in life form a blueprint of how a child will form relationships in the future.

Attachment, as the first social system to develop, provides security for the infant. In situations of complex developmental trauma, early difficulties within the child's primary relationship establish a pattern of mistrust of others. Attachment theory posits that these relational behaviors will persist throughout life; however, research has shown promise in utilizing manualized curriculums and strategies that are useful in modifying relational behaviors (Blitz & Lee, 2015; Day et al. 2015; National Child Traumatic Stress Network and National Center for PTSD, 2006; Purvis, et al., 2013; Substance Abuse and Mental Health Services Administration, 2014; Schwartz, 2016).

Personal Toll of Trauma

As previously noted, trauma strikes children from many directions within their ecological systems. Despite the widespread occurrence of PTEs, children, teachers and society at large are underprepared to deal with the burden these events place on them. In situations of acute trauma, for example, the occurrence of a natural disaster, such as Hurricane Katrina, or a human-made tragedy, such as the Sandy Hook school shooting, the trauma experienced by all is highly visible. In these instances the community, the nation, and sometimes the world rises to support the victims of such events. In this way, at least initially, the children and community pull together to address each other's needs in the short-term.

Unlike large-scale events, however, chronic complex developmental trauma is sometimes suffered in private. School systems and teachers go unaware of the child's experience of PTEs and, therefore, make faulty hypotheses about the learning and behavioral difficulties displayed. For example, one researcher found that teachers described students affected by trauma as appearing unmotivated and disengaged; in reality the children's "...concerns outside the classroom overwhelmed them" (Sitler, 2008, p. 119).

Researchers reporting the observed behavioral manifestations of children who had experienced trauma include both internalizing and externalizing characteristics. Internalizing behaviors noted included passivity, lack of interest in the future, inability to concentrate, spacing out, frequent absences, poor work habits, and coming to school less ready to learn. Some negative externalizing behaviors displayed by children who had experienced trauma include verbal or physical aggression, breaking classroom rules, refusing assistance, bullying, and involvement with the juvenile justice system (Blitz & Lee, 2015; Mallett, 2013; Sitler, 2008; Wright, 2014).

These negative behavioral characteristics in response to trauma make sense given that humans have an automatic stress response system; making children's behavior in response to a perceived threat out of their normal control (Wright, 2014). This automatic stress response initiates responses that are characterized as fight – flight – freeze. The specific response to a situation will vary based on the individual child's psychological make-up, the environmental conditions, the perceived threat, and the instantaneous analysis of the situation. Children may often appear impulsive and out of control, or withdrawn because the stress response system responds automatically, without engaging a cognitive analysis of the situation (Wright, 2014).

In addition to behavioral manifestations of trauma, children also experience psychological effects related to PTEs. These effects impact thoughts about themselves – poor feelings of self-worth, expectations of others – beliefs that adults will always let them down, and difficulty with the ability to engage in learning behaviors – low levels of attention, concentration, memory and organizational skills. Research has examined children's perceptions in response to trauma and found that the typical hypervigilance, being on guard and suspicious, is activated even when dangers are not present.

Twelve Core Concepts of Trauma

In 2007, a task force was engaged to examine the conceptual understandings of PTEs as they pertain to children. The National Child Traumatic Stress Network formed the Core Curriculum Task Force to identify the guiding principles for engaging in trauma-informed care (National Child Traumatic Stress Network Core Curriculum on Childhood Trauma Task Force, 2012). It is important to understand and act on these fundamental principles in an effort to help children recover and overcome the experienced trauma. The 12 Core Concepts for Trauma-Informed Care developed by the task force are paraphrased and summarized below (National Child Traumatic

Stress Network Core Curriculum on Childhood Trauma Task Force, 2012).

- Traumatic experiences are inherently complex. Children display subjective responses to traumatizing events with chronic exposure and perpetrating events by primary caregivers constituting highly complex experiences of trauma.
- Trauma occurs within a broad context that includes children's personal characteristics, life experiences, and current circumstances. The broad ecology that encompasses both child intrinsic and extrinsic factors influence the appraisal of PTEs in regard to the events.
- Traumatic events often generate secondary adversities, life changes, and distressing reminders in children's daily lives. Changes produced by trauma can tax the coping resources of the child, family, and community.
- Children can exhibit a wide range of reactions to trauma and loss. Child psychological factors and ecological contexts influence how the specific trauma is experienced.
- Danger and safety are core concerns in the lives of traumatized children. Ensuring children's physical safety is important but may not be sufficient to alleviate fears.
- Traumatic experiences affect the family and broader care-giving systems. PTEs can seriously disrupt attachment relationships. Supporting care-giving systems are necessary for effective intervention.
- Protective and promotive factors can reduce the adverse impact of trauma. The presence and strength of protective child intrinsic (e.g. self-esteem) and extrinsic factors (e.g. social supportive network) can enhance children's ability to recover.
- Trauma and post-trauma adversities can strongly influence development. Experiences of trauma can impact the attainment of developmental milestones. Timelines associated with developmental milestones can either regress or accelerate demonstrated behaviors.
- Developmental neurobiology underlies children's reactions to traumatic experiences. Evolving brain structures, neurophysiological pathways, and the neuroendocrine system

are linked to children's capacities to appraise and respond to danger.

- Culture is closely interwoven with traumatic experiences, response and recovery. Culture influences the meaning ascribed to traumatic events as well as the responses of children and families to the trauma.

- Challenges to the social contract, including legal and ethical issues, affect trauma response and recovery. Traumatic experiences are a violation of child, family, and community expectations; how justice is served can impact post-trauma adjustment.

- Working with trauma-exposed children can evoke distress in providers that make it more difficult for them to provide good care. Good self-care is an essential component of working with traumatized children; personal memories of experiences of trauma and loss can be evoked while supporting others' recovery.

Trauma-Informed Curriculums

The concept of trauma-informed care has spread throughout the mental-health community in response to the identification of the pervasive nature of PTEs. In extension, other agencies and areas within ecological systems have embraced the need to examine how the experience of trauma affects children's life trajectories. For example, Mallett (2014) examined the connection between victimization, education difficulties, and mental health disorders in a sample of juvenile offenders. Results of his investigation found specifically that between 26 and 60 percent of court-involved adolescents have trauma histories in regard to maltreatment, representing a significant concern for all those involved. In this investigation, all types of childhood maltreatment – physical abuse, sexual abuse, and neglect were linked to later antisocial behavior and court involvement; thus, research is clear that all types of chronic trauma related to maltreatment have a significant impact on juvenile offending behavior.

Mallett (2014) also established the link between maltreatment, juvenile offending and school difficulties; demonstrating that children with histories of chronic maltreatment experience cognitive and language delays, higher school absenteeism rates, as well as higher rates of learning disability and mental health disorder identification. The link between trauma, school difficulties and court involvement is clear, emphasizing the necessity for the coordination of efforts across "youth-caring systems" (Mallett, 2014, p.382). One trauma-informed curriculum that was tested in a school for court-referred youth is called the Heart of Teaching and Learning (HTL). HTL is a manualized curriculum whose "... ultimate goal is to help the students view themselves as worthy and lovable and to perceive relationships as positive and rewarding" (Day et al., 2015).

School-based curriculums devoted to supporting those who have experienced traumatizing events have been developed and examined under various circumstances. One such standardized curriculum that holds significant potential for positive effect was developed during a summer camp for adopted and foster children called the Trust-Based Relational Intervention (TBRI). This curriculum has continued to be refined over the course of 20 years of implementation. TBRI principles address childhood ecological, and physiological needs through 1) empowerment, 2) connection, and 3) correction. Under these three pillars, teachers provide attention to physical needs, attachment needs, and behavioral needs (Purvis et al., 2013).

Teachers working from this framework ensure that student's basic needs are met, that relational and attachment needs are met, and that self-regulation, appropriate boundaries, and healthy behaviors are taught. Providers of TBRI affirm, "TBRI addresses all major issues that are linked with complex developmental trauma and has been adapted for a variety of settings..." (Purvis et al., 2013, p.376).

One other curriculum focused on the mental health of children in elementary school is called Unconditional Education (Schwartz, 2016). Unconditional education starts by training teachers about trauma; specifically, examining the effects of trauma on the brain, and the behavioral manifestations of traumatized children. The goal is to keep the children in the classroom, to build positive, trusting relationships, develop individual interventions, and to remind the child that the experienced trauma is not the child's fault. The creators of Unconditional Education set out to create a sustainable, whole school approach that ultimately would become part of the culture of the school. Results from the evaluation of the implemented program demonstrated positive results. Although it took a full year to gain teacher buy-in of the curriculum, the school administration prioritized the curriculum thereby giving teachers the message that the curriculum was an important part of the school culture.

Trauma-Informed Practice

The Substance Abuse and Mental Health Services Administration (SAMHSA) (2014) provided four key assumptions for all organizations that want to put into effect a trauma-informed approach to working with children. SAMHSA states that all individuals within the system must have a basic understanding of trauma – what it is, how it impacts individuals, etc. Those same individuals need to be trained on how to recognize trauma-impacted people. One suggestion was to provide organization-wide trauma screenings. Furthermore, the organization has to have policies and practices in place to respond to trauma when identified. Finally, the practices of the organization should avoid re-traumatization of individuals. Essentially, when followed, the four assumptions detailed by SAMHSA put into place an organization that sends the message that trauma sensitivity is part of the organizational culture. Similarly, schools must establish a trauma-informed culture at every level in order to support those children within the school recover from traumatic experiences. This is similar to what occurs at the Universal Level in common school-based programming such as Response to Intervention and Positive Behavior Intervention Supports. Within both school programs, the entire school has a mutual vision of the goal of the program and all individuals in the school work to support student success.

Rather than viewing children who have experienced trauma as being 'at-risk', it is important to understand the adaptive aspects of the children's behaviors. The internalizing and externalizing behaviors demonstrated at school and in the classroom may have kept those children safe in other circumstances. Instead of labeling these children as learning disabled, attention-deficit hyperactivity disordered, or emotionally disturbed, teachers can help children heal their trauma through fostering positive relationships, scaffolding effective transitions, and creating a supportive learning environment.

It is important to recognize that a teacher's failure to respond to a child in a validating way can re-traumatize the child; moving them away from understanding that the school is a safe and protected environment. "Reframing the work of teaching from labeling and rescuing students to recognizing and building on the inherent strengths is a first step in helping children with traumatic backgrounds to experience success and feel pride" (Wright, 2014, p. 92).

All teachers, regardless of whether their school adopts a school-wide trauma-informed approach, can implement six principles within their classroom setting in order to establish a trauma-informed teaching practice. The six principles, recommended by SAMHSA (2014) with strategies suggested by Wright (2014) are as follows:

- Safety. Provide for both the physical safety as well as emotional safety of the children. Remember the children being served must define their own feelings of safety. Teachers can reinforce the understanding, through words and actions, that the classroom is a safe place both physically and emotionally.

- Trustworthiness and Transparency. Children must have a clear understanding of the procedures, the structure of the activities of the day, and the rules and expectations. With transparency and consistency, trust in self and others can be developed. Teachers can facilitate this by discussing, rehearsing and revisiting the expectations and rules for the classroom. Children will internalize this structure and as long as the teacher is consistent, the children can count on the classroom consistency. Teachers can also post a schedule of daily activities or classroom rules for students to refer to.

- Peer Support. Systems of support, provided by family members or others who have experienced similar events, provides for a community of survivors; allowing children to tell their own stories when and if they want to can help to promote classroom empathy and indicates to the child that what they say has value. Teachers can show interest in children and their lives by asking questions and remembering the details of what had been shared.

- Collaboration and Mutuality. Healing happens through relationships. Working with others in multiple contexts, when everyone is functioning on a similar level, can reinforce the benefits of relationships. Teachers can use direct instruction to help children learn how to work effectively with others. Teachers can model strategies and students can role-play in order to learn essential skills. Teachers can engage regularly with children in warm, one-on-one conversations.

- Empowerment, Voice, and Choice. Children's strengths are recognized and built on in an effort to promote resilience within the child. Those strengths are then utilized to foster resiliency. Teachers can allow children time and space to calm down in their own way when upset. Teachers can provide direct instruction on emotions, teaching how to identify feelings, as well as naming and validating various emotions in the classroom.

- Cultural, Historical and Gender Issues. All cultural, ethnic, religious, and gender groups should feel welcome in the classroom setting. Each child is viewed as an individual with unique qualities that are valued. Teachers can make sure to include all perspectives in discussions, classroom readings, stories, and work. Teachers can select books utilized in the classroom that are inclusive of all groups.

Conclusion

Potentially traumatizing events (PTEs) are more commonly experienced by children than most people would like to believe. In a community survey of children and adolescents, more than two-thirds of those sampled reported experiencing a traumatic event before their 16th birthday (APA, 2008). Trauma is a sudden, unpredictable event that elicits fear and an automatic stress-response in an individual. Trauma can be a short-time, one-event experience, or it can be a chronic and ongoing adversely stressful experience. In children, the timing of the traumatic experience is important to note as it can trigger secondary symptoms such as behavioral regression or acceleration. This complex developmental trauma can ultimately have far-reaching life consequences such as school failure and juvenile justice involvement if children are not provided with the necessary supports to recover from the traumatic experience.

As children spend a great deal of time in schools each day, schools can become a safe haven for children who have experienced trauma. Teachers who have gained an understanding of a trauma-informed approach to teaching can provide the consistency and structure that children need in order to ameliorate the hypervigilance they experience as an aftermath to trauma. Trauma-informed teaching has at its core the nurturance of feelings of safety and attachment in the children who have experienced trauma. Although it is ideal to have a systems-wide trauma-informed approach that utilizes a standard curriculum, teachers who do not have administrative backing may want to engage in trauma-informed teaching practices within their own classrooms.

Points to Remember

- *Many children in school settings have experienced at least one potentially traumatizing event (PTE), while others demonstrate characteristics of complex developmental trauma. This makes schools a perfect place to provide a trauma-informed approach to teaching.*
- *Children's automatic stress response fight – flight – freeze, engages without the child's conscious control; it is sometimes true that the child's behavior is out of their volitional control.*
- *Children's outward behavioral displays such as withdrawal or physical aggression, and psychological characteristics such as disrupted attention, memory and organizational capacities, are typical responses to coping with traumatizing events.*
- *The key classroom practices of a trauma-informed teaching approach include providing a physically and emotionally safe environment for all students, and developing a warm and caring relationship with the children.*
- *Teachers who understand trauma-informed teaching practices are less likely to misinterpret demonstrated behavioral and social-emotional difficulties as intentional. Trauma-informed teachers respond with calm reassurance in order to de-escalate the persistent fear traumatized children manifest.*

References

American Psychological Association Presidential Task Force on Posttraumatic Stress Disorder and Trauma in Children and Adolescents. (2008). *Children and trauma: Update for mental health professionals.* Retrieved from http://www.apa.org/pi/families/resources/children-trauma-update.aspx

Bartlett, J.D., Smith, S., & Bringewatt, E. (2017, April). Helping young children who have experienced trauma: Policies and strategies for early care and education. Child Trends Publication No. 2017-19. *National Center for Children in Poverty,* Columbia University, NY. Retrieved from http://www.ddcf.org/globalassets/17-0428-helping-young-children-who-have-experienced-trauma.pdf

Blitz, L.V, &Lee, Y. (2015). Trauma-informed methods to enhance school-based bullying prevention initiatives: An emerging model. *Journal of Aggression, Maltreatment & Trauma,* 24. 20-40. DOI:10.1080/10926771.2015.982238

Bronfenbrenner, U. (1986). Ecology of the family as a context for human development: Research Perspectives. *Developmental Psychology,* 22, 723-742. DOI:10.1037/0012-1649.22.6.723

Day, A.G., Somers, C.L., Baroni, B.A, West, S.D. Sanders, L., & Peterson, C.D. (2015). Evaluation of a trauma-informed school intervention with girls in a residential facility school: Student perceptions of school environment. Journal of Aggression, Maltreatment & Trauma, 24. 1086-1105. DOI:10.1080/10926771.2015.1079279

Deihl, L.M. (2013, November). Children and trauma: How schools can help with healing. *The Brown University Child and Adolescent Behavior Letter,* 29 (11), 1-7. Retrieved from http://www.childadolescentbehavior.com/Article-Detail/children-and-trauma-how-schools-can-help-with-healing.aspx

Litz, B.T., Miller, M.W., Ruef, A.M., & McTeague, L.M. (2002). *Exposure to trauma in adults. Approaches for Specific Psychological Problems.* New York, NY: The Guildford Press.

Mallett, C.A. (2014). Youthful offending and delinquency: The comorbid impact of maltreatment, mental health problems, and learning disabilities. *Journal of Child and Adolescent Social Work,* 31. 369-392. DOI:10.1007/s10560-013-032303

National Child Traumatic Stress Network Core Curriculum on Childhood Trauma Task Force. (2012). *The 12 core concepts: Concepts for understanding traumatic stress responses in children and families. Core Curriculum on Childhood Trauma.* Los Angeles, CA, and Durham, NC: UCLA-Duke University National Center for Child Traumatic Stress. National Child Traumatic Stress Network and National Center for PTSD, Psychological First Aid: Field Operations Guide, (2nd ed.), July 2006. Retrieved from www.nctsn.org and www.ncptsd.va.gov

O'Neill, L., Guenette, F., & Kitchenham, A. (2010). 'Am I safe here and do you like me?' Understanding complex trauma and attachment disruption in the classroom. *British Journal of Special Education*, 37 (4), 190-197. DOI:10.1111/j.1467-8578.2010.00477

Purvis, K.B., Cross, D.R., Dansereau, D.F., & Parris, S.R. (2013). Trust-based relational intervention (TBRI): A systemic approach to complex developmental trauma. *Child & Youth Services*, 34. 360-386. DOI:10.1080/0145935X.2013.859906

Substance Abuse and Mental Health Services Administration. (2014) *SAMHSA's concept of Trauma and guidance for a trauma-informed approach. HHS Publication No.* (SMA)14-4884. Rockville, MD: Substance Abuse and Mental Health Services Administration.

Schwartz, K. (2016, June). How trauma-informed teaching builds a sense of safety and care. Mind/Shift. How we Will Learn. Retrieved from http://ww2.kqed.org/mindshift/2016/06/06/how-trauma-informed-teaching-builds-a-sense-of-safety-and-care.

Sitler, H.C. (2009, January/February). Teaching with awareness: The hidden effects of trauma onlearning. *The Clearing House*, 82 (3), 119-123. Retrieved from https://eric.ed.gov/?id=EJ821074

Wright, T. (2014, November). Too scared to learn. Teaching young children who have experienced trauma. *Young Children*, 88-93. Retrieved from http://www.naeyc.org/yc/pastissues/2014/november

Chapter 9

Cultural Consideration: Promoting Emotional Well-Being in Students with Learning Disabilities

Nicholas D. Young, *American International College,*
Elizabeth Jean, *Endicott College,*
and Anne E. Mead, *Danbury Public Schools*

Schools are becoming increasingly more diverse as families with school-aged children move from countries outside the United States, necessitating a new proficiency in recognizing the cultural beliefs and value systems of new clientele (Quinton, 2013; RTI, n.d.; Wells, Fox, & Cordova-Cobo, 2016). Though schools and their educators are well trained in testing that identifies students with learning disabilities, the growing population of students whose native language is not English can be troublesome for educators who are testing and designing programs for students with presumed learning disabilities (Villegas-Gutierrez, 2015).

As non-English speaking students struggle with achieving literacy standards, the determination and/or classification of learning disabilities may be over-identified due to the population's complexity with literacy competencies (Gonzalez & Artiles, 2015). An additional issue is the disparity of educator diversity versus the families they work with. The majority of today's educators come from European-American middle-class families and lack the knowledge of working with diverse families (Futterman, 2015).

In most schools, only a few educators reflect minorities and even fewer speech-language pathologists represent minorities (Lo, 2012). Though educator preparation programs have strong curricula in teaching pedagogy, minimal coursework in understanding diversity is offered, which leaves staff at a loss for designing culturally responsive classrooms and teaching practices (Mead, 2017).

The growing population of students from different countries and those with learning disabilities demonstrate fewer relationships and social functioning (Martins, Cummings, O'Neill, & Strnadova, 2017). It is imperative that teachers be prepared by having the knowledge to build environments and curricula that support the emotional well-being of students (Quinton, 2013).

Educators who serve children and families need to think beyond the word 'diversity' as meaning 'differences'; rather the focus must be to create an inclusive environment in all activities undertaken by a school, agency or organization.

In any discussion regarding cultural differences, a clear connection between diversity and inclusiveness must be made. Inclusiveness is offering the family a sense of belonging and connectedness, allowing for natural context and environments, encouraging families to understand a wide range of abilities and the continuum of development, and policies and procedures that encourage all children to have equity in opportunities that support their growth and development (Bienia, 2016).

Understanding Families

Each family comes to school with personal traditions, educational beliefs, and values. These views influence how parents interact with their children, educational professionals, and their expectations for learning skills. While schools have their own culture, families bring with them their own ethnicity, beliefs and traditions (Futterman, 2015; Villegas-Gutierrez, 2015).

During the last 25 years, families from other countries coming to the United States have increased exponentially, therefore it is imperative that educators understand the backgrounds of all families; what motivates them as well as how their cultural and familial backgrounds influence the decisions they make about their children (Quinton, 2013; More, Hart, Cheatham, 2013). Though it is the intention of educators to have inclusive classrooms that reflect diversity of the students, tensions exist when there is a mismatching of cultural expectations (Olivos, et al., 2010).

Understanding families, the meaning of diversity, and inclusiveness are the pillars that lead educators to think about the emotional well-being of students and how this overall impression affects confidence, success as a learner, and relationships formed (Sanchez,

2017). The pillars precede the ability to form relationships with typical and atypical peers.

All children, no matter their ability, have families that should advocate for their child's autonomy to access activities, develop relatedness, and competence to keep pace with peers as they participate in global activities (Bailey, 2012). Educators who understand families, and the diversity they bring to programs through their children, have more inclusiveness in their classrooms that lead to students' well-being (Sanchez, 2017).

It is imperative for educators to know and understand the children and families to which they are assigned; to recognize what motivates them, their cultural and familial backgrounds, and how they make decisions about their children (Quinton, 2013; Kozleski, n.d.). Many families who are faced with the realization that their child may have a learning disability go through a grieving process. Well prepared educators are able to support families through this process when they know how a particular family functions, and what cultural beliefs and values are instilled in the family; thus, the family will find the process more fulfilling and the outcomes more satisfying (Lo, 2012).

No matter the origins of the family, each comes to the educational setting protective of their children and ready to participate in decision-making at a level they are comfortable with (Kozleski, n.d.). Families differ in their ability to be part of the decision-making process and educators need to be aware of how to work with them. All decisions, whether program related or not, need to be made in the best interest of the child (Mead, 2017). Though institutions are thought to be school-centric, keeping the child at the center of all decision-making enables the family to better understand what is appropriate and how the decision will affect their youngster (Gillanders, McKinney and Ritchie, 2012).

Protective factors are those strategies that parents use to reduce risks for their child to experience undesirable outcomes. Protective factors imposed by parents may inhibit a child with learning disabilities to be fully immersed in opportunities that support their emotional well-being. Whereas, parents who realize the prospect that activities such as academic interventions or therapeutic recreation, such as equestrian therapy, the arts, or music therapy offers children a chance to have positive outcomes (Bailey, 2012; Schweizer, 2014; McFerran & Rickson, 2014).

An example of protective factors in the Hispanic population exhibits itself as a psychological respect for, and closeness of, family (Telzer, Gonales, Fuligna, 2014). Often times, it is the expectation of the extended family members to support one another that enables parents to have a higher level of parenting self-efficacy and thus allows their children better opportunities for activities that contribute to their well-being (Telzer, Gonales, Fuligna, 2014).

Protective factors may inhibit a student with learning disabilities from having a parent's full approval to take advantage of all learning opportunities (Cohen, Holloway, Dominguez-Pereto, & Kupperman, 2014). Educators should seek out the support and protective factors that extended families possess (Cohen, et al., 2014).

Educators can be "powerful and effective sources of support" (Cohen, et al., 2014, p. 342) when they learn about family belief and protective systems that leverage additional assistance from extended family members. Changing a parent's mindset to allow educators to assist them with learning about their beliefs and protective systems is often difficult to do; however, a well-trained teacher is able to accomplish when given the proper tools (Mead, 2017).

Barriers and Boundaries

Significant barriers to engagement in meetings and conferences include a lack of trust between schools and families as well as linguistic barriers that prevent communication (Henderson & Mapp, 2010). Though all families understand the importance of engaging in their child's school and communicating to share information, these barriers often negate successful programs. Communication with lower income families is often of a negative nature about missed assignments, learning needs, or behavioral issues and may involve an interpreter who may not be well-versed in the terms and language used with children with learning disabilities (Suarez-Orozco, Yoshikawa, Teranishi and Suarez-Orozco, 2011).

Other barriers that impact engagement with schools are feelings of intimidation or a fear of deportation on the part of the family members. While many families may be hesitant to engage with schools due to these fears, others approach education with lower expectations due to lacking social resources such as the ability to be full partners with their child's class (Gonzalez, Borders, Hines, Villaba and Henderson, 2013).

Some parents may feel they don't have the knowledge or the ability to engage with their child's school due to their lack of knowledge about special education systems and the planning meetings that educators take part in to provide education services for their child (Suarez-Orozco, Yoshikawa, Teranishi and Suarez-Orozco, 2011). Furthermore, knowledge, behaviors, and cultural barriers are factors that discourage parents from seeking opportunities to participate in their children's school (Futterman, 2015).

Embedded within Hispanic culture are clear boundaries between school and home. At home, Hispanic families teach their children about religion and citizenship while schools focus on academics (Raty, 2011). Hispanic families may not feel they have the ability or insight to impact the educational process or are capable of being a valuable member at meetings; however, this could not be further from the truth (Ruiz, 2012). Schools and educators with an understanding of these boundaries and who are aware of their student's home culture help achieve a higher level of school and parent engagement and are able to build better partnerships (Raty, 2011).

A first step when assessing culturally and linguistically diverse students who may present with learning disabilities is to use Response to Intervention (RtI) (RTI Action Network, n.d.). Used in conjunction with the parents, this tool assesses the student's ability to perform academically as well as show emotional and behavioral resiliency (Villegas-Gutierrez, 2015). Ensuring that students are not misdiagnosed due to "byproducts of acculturation" (Villegas-Gutierrez, 2015) is an important step in the process of identification and finding appropriate services.

Cultural Connections

Children develop cultural connections with others through their experiences with the world. It is important for children to have a strong sense of their own cultural history and traditions as a means to building a positive cultural identity (Commonwealth of Australia, 2013). Within this framework children learn to fit into two cultures and make sense of the different expectations.

Typically developing children can make sense of two competing cultures simultaneously; however, children with learning disabilities often don't understand the nuances (Martins, Cummings, O'Neill, & Strnadova, 2017). Teaching strategies that educators use should take into consideration the student's limited understanding about their culture and embed techniques that are relevant to the child's level of understanding of their native culture and that cultural expectation in the U.S. (Martins, Cummings, O'Neill, & Strnadova, 2017).

Well-Being Defined

Well-being is defined as "the state of being comfortable, healthy, or happy in every aspect in your life" (Office of Disease Prevention and Health Promotion, 2016). This affects all areas of life including relationships, diet and exercise, sleep and leisure, self-esteem and a sense of belonging (Office of Disease Prevention and Health Promotion, 2016). People with learning disabilities are often shut out from activities and left with very limited opportunities for beneficial leisure; thus, it is important to provide these opportunities to improve their quality of life and well-being (Sanchez, 2017).

Positive relationships within schools have frequently been identified as central to student well-being (McFerran & Shoemaker, 2013). Therapeutic recreation and interventions generate "social, emotional, physical, psychological, or spiritual change" (Hawkins, Cory, McGuire, & Allen, 2012, p.1) as a means to improve all aspects of quality of life. Students whose families take advantage of, and are supportive of, a diverse menu of recreational activities are better prepared for life and their well-being is more fulfilling.

Creating Positive Environments

A positive environment created by classroom teachers and schools fosters growth in families and children by making connectedness to the community more beneficial. Families who report they feel connectedness to the child's school community have better learning results (Kozleski, n.d.). Additionally, connectedness and a feeling of belonging aids in creating and understanding the goals that families have for their children (Sanchez, 2017).

The educator who spends time learning about the cultural norms of their families displays relevance that reflects the students' backgrounds (Quinton, 2013). Areas in the room or close to the room where families can congregate to talk to one another build a sense of connectedness between school and home. More so, classroom space where children can spend time together doing mutually beneficial activities gives them the time to grow connectedness to one another (Mead, 2017).

In typical students, the development stage termed 'observer' happens early in a child's life, under 18 months; however, for a child with learning disabilities this phase may last a lifetime or be used intermittently as a way to assess situations (Sanchez, 2017). Pictures hung throughout the classroom of differing emotions enables teachers to quickly help children identify how and why they are feeling a certain way or to provide support for their needs (Coyne, Kame'enui, & Carnine, 2011). Areas within classrooms or centers should vary between highly active and quiet. Quiet areas give children the opportunity to rest and observe what others are doing in the room (Jamison, Forston, & Stanton-Chapman, 2012).

Pairing of Children for Instruction and Recreation

It is educators' responsibility to develop emotionally supportive classrooms and provide instruction that is tailored to individual needs (Merritt, Wanless, Rimm-Kaufman, & Peugh, 2012). Children in classes without well-developed social-emotional skills need differentiated instruction to improve skills. Children with more mature skills can be paired up with those who need extra support (Jamison, et al., 2012). Identified children will need more support and most likely will not seek out playmates. Educators can take this opportunity to move a child within close proximity to a child with more advanced skills (Jamison, et al., 2012).

Social and emotional development in children is defined in terms of temperament styles, stages of development and attachment theory (Hong & Park, 2012). Integrated into this development includes children learning about the world around them, development of appropriate language to get their needs resolved, and the attachment they have with other significant people. Healthy attachment with others encourages students to play and work with others in an age-appropriate way; however, students with learning disabilities may need support in this area (Brumariu, 2015; Hong & Park, 2012).

Therapeutic recreation is a wide range of activities designed for an individual or a group of like individuals. Activities are confidence builders; therapeutic music, art or swimming increases the capacity of an individual and helps builds their autonomy (Esseff, 2016). Learning opportunities through recreational therapy builds a child's self-confidence, development of socialization skills, emotions management and impulse control that affect lifelong well-being (Hawkins et al., 2012). Arts therapy helps a student develop self-awareness and self-esteem skills, and a child's image of him or herself in relation to others (Hawkins, et al., 2012).

Art as an intervention. Art in itself is self-expression for a child who cannot express thoughts in words; however, students with learning disabilities and behavioral, emotional, and psychological issues also find art soothing (Schweizer, Knorth, & Spreen; 2014). It has a proven track record as a successful treatment and can be used as a sign of communication for an alert educator to determine its meaning (Hawkins, et al., 2012).

The American Therapeutic Recreation Association (2014) suggests that art therapy develops coping skills by reducing stress and develops interpersonal skills when the student is paired with others. The use of tactile and visual experiences build changes to the child's schema and "can stimulate change of behavior and integration of cognitive-sensoric and kinesthetic experiences and behaviors" (Schweizer, et al., 2014, p. 2).

Through different forms of art children learn about materials, some indigenous to their countries of origin, and by creating their own product develop self-confidence (Schweizer et al., 2014). Students who participate in taking tools out, putting them away, following directions and following through on their own are learning executive functioning (EF) skills (Blasco, Saxton, & Gerrie, 2014).

Though executive functioning skills are considered an advanced skill in which information is organized in such a way that planned behaviors are the outcome (Blasco, et al., 2014). Children with learning disabilities often lack solid executive functioning skills that affects their self-determination and interpersonal relationships; thus, it is imperative that all children learn some form of this skill as executive functioning is rudimentary to other learning (Martin, et al., 2017).

Music Therapy. Like art, music uses many of the learning domains that a child with learning disabilities may not have the capacity to use during their normal school day (McFerran & Rickson, 2014). In many cases, individual student plans are written that identify learning goals but exclude areas outside of academic learning. Children with learning disabilities have favorable results when the priority of developing meaningful relations are a focus of their learning plans (McFerran & Shoemaker, 2013).

Families and music therapists report that the relationship built between the interventionist and the student is dynamic, and often not thought of as an important component of the engagement between the two (McFerran & Shoemaker, 2013). Children with severe learning disabilities have the "capacity for relationships, development of personality, lifestyle preferences and emotional development, all are fundamental markers of well-being" (Stern, 2010, p. 89).

Music produces a positive mood through neurological impulses in the brain that calms students and build relationships with others. Furthermore, music can be treated as a universal language understood by all cultures (Henderson, Cain, Istvandity & Lakhani, 2016). In schools where academics are the primary focus, families from other countries are often confused (McFerran & Shoemaker, 2013). Music therapy or music time with students who have severe learning disabilities, and their families, becomes a way that culture can be shared and common ground can be found.

Reading and Dogs. Students who lack proficiency in reading at an early age, in most cases never reach proficiency compared to their non-disabled peers (Lenihan, McCobb, Diurba, Linder, & Freeman, 2016). Additionally, they have lower self-esteem, withdraw for other activities that can lead to isolation and depression, and a high rate of school drop-out (Lenihan, McCobb, Diurba, Linder, & Freeman, 2016). A recent study (le Roux, Swartz, & Swart, 2014) suggests that students who have reading difficulties as young children are seriously impacted both short and long-term in the areas of learning experiences and emotional development.

To support reading skill development in students with learning disabilities, several studies (le Roux et al., 2014; Lenihan, et al., 2016) found that human contact, as well as a relationship with an animal made a significant difference in student outcomes. For example, when students read to a therapy dog, there was an increase in word usage, increase in free speech, and decreased stress levels (le Roux et al., 2014; Lenihan, et al., 2016). Students were more willing to read out loud, which increases fluency, to an animal as the child exhibits no fear and there was no reprisal from the animal (le Roux, et al., 2014). Educators found an increase in student outcomes while increasing their self-confidence and willingness to be vocal (Lenihan, et al., 2016).

Direct Instruction. Findings from a recent report (Wylie & Bonne, 2015) suggest that more than half the principals surveyed found direct instruction the best tool for teaching strategies to students with learning disabilities about how to manage "their feelings, self-management skills, dealing with others, health and physical education, transitional activities, co-curricular activities, and career choices" (p.56). In another study (Martins, Cummings, O'Neill, & Strnadova, 2017), students who received direct instruction on personal and interpersonal agency developed more self-determination that led to better outcomes. Student choice was found to be of higher quality; however, over-confidence led to poor academic outcomes due to limited metacognitive abilities (Martins, Cummings, O'Neill, & Strnadova, 2017).

For many students with LD, direction instruction uses a skills-based approach to literacy regardless of the social context and the role of culture in which the student is immersed in with his or her family (Klingner, Boele, Linan-Thompson, & Rodriguez, 2014). This approach leaves the instruction devoid of any cultural considerations; however, there are educators that use a sociocultural approach to literacy and learning that takes into consideration the cultural context that the student is immersed in and has minimal consideration for a struggling learner (Gonzalez & Artiles, 2015). These two approaches, skill based and sociocultural context, need to tie their philosophical underpinnings to one that meets the needs of all learners.

Conclusion

When families from culturally diverse communities attempt to connect with schools in an effort to help their child with a learning disability, it can be frustrating and lead to a lack of trust with the school. Often this can be mitigated by a culturally proficient educational staff who makes an extra effort to learn about and understand the families they serve. Educators must learn about the values, beliefs and traditions while gaining the trust of the families in their care. They must also find ways to show families that their home culture is important. This can be accomplished by providing areas in or near the classroom that are quiet spaces or have items common to the cultures of the families being served that children can access.

When a parent discovers their child has a learning disability they may be confused or upset. It is helpful if the educator has a working relationship with the family and can help them come to terms with this realization. Once parents feel comfortable, they are likely to remove barriers and protective factors in order to let their child thrive in a new environment with special education services that directly and positively impact the student and his or her well-being.

Regardless, or perhaps in spite of cultural differences, family and educator are bound together to support the child with a learning disability; however, this difficult task begins with the educator. Helping the family to understand the nuances and requirements of special education and keeping the child at the center of all decisions, ensures his or her well-being and emotional needs are being met.

Points to Remember

- *Diversity must be seen as more than simply differences but rather as an inclusive environment in all activities undertaken by an organization, agency or school*

- *A premium should be placed on understanding a family's cultural traditions, values and beliefs in order to connect to and support the family throughout the special education process.*

- *Protective factors are strategies that reduce risks and undesirable outcomes. They must be mitigated in order for a child with learning disabilities to thrive.*

- *Barriers to engage families in the special education process include lack of trust, linguistic frustrations, feelings of intimidation or fear, and lack of knowledge.*

- *Creating positive environments such as recreational interventions, pairing children and quiet spaces, can help students increase a personal sense of well-being.*

References

American Therapeutic Recreation Association. (2016). *What is RT/TR?* Retrieved from http://www.atra-online/what/FAQ

Bailey, G, (2012). *Emotional well-being for children with special needs and disabilities: a guide for practitioners.* Thousand Oaks, CA: Sage.

Bienia, E. J. (2016). *Preschool partnerships: How teachers make sense of their experiences.* (Doctoral dissertation). Retrieved from https://repository.library.northeastern.edu/files/neu:cj82nc92v

Blasco, P.M., Saxton, S., & Gerrie, M. (2014). The little brain that could: Understanding executive function in early childhood. *Young Exceptional Children, 17*(3), 3-18. Retrieved from https://eric.ed.gov/?id=EJ1040106

Cohen, S. R., Holloway, S. D., Dominguez-Pareto, I., & Kupperman, M. (2014). Receiving or believing in family support? Contributors to the life quality of Latino and non-Latino families of children with intellectual disability. *Journal of Intellectual Disability Research, 58*(4). doi: 10.1111/jir.12016

Coyne, M.D., Kame-enui, E.J., Carnine, D.W. (2011). *Effective teaching strategies that accommodate diverse learners.* Saddle River, NJ: Pearson.

Esseff, S. L. (2016). *Benefits of therapeutic recreation for young adults with special needs.* from http://digitalcommons.csumb.edu/caps_thes_all/29

Futterman, L. (2015). *Beyond the classroom: The impact of culture on the classroom.* Retrieved from http://www.miamiherald.com/news/local/community/miami-dade/community-voices/article36727782.html

Gillanders, C., McKinney, M., Ritchie, S. (2012). What kind of school would you like for your children? Exploring minority mothers' beliefs to promote home-school partnerships. *Early Childhood Education Journal, 40*(5), 285 - 294. DOI: 10.1007/s10643-012-05140

Gonzalez, T., & Artiles, A. J. (2015). Reframing venerable standpoints about language and learning differences: The need for research on the literate lives of Latina/o language minority students. *Journal of Multilingual Education Research, 6,* 9-34. Retrieved from http://fordham.bepress.com/cgi/viewcontent.cgi?article=1076&context=jmer

Henderson, S., Cain, M., Istvandity, L., & Lakhani, A. (2016). The role of music participation in positive health and wellbeing outcomes for migrant populations: A systematic review. *The Psychology of Music,* 1-20. DOI: 10.1177/0305735616665910.

Hong, Y.R. & Park, J.S. (2012). *Impact of attachment, temperament and parenting on human development.* DOI: 10.3345/kjp.2012.55.12.449.

Jamison, K. R., Forston, L. D., & Stanton-Chapman, T. L. (2012), Encouraging social skill development through play in early childhood special education classrooms. *Young Exceptional Children,* 15(2), 3-19. DOI: 10.1177/1096250611435422

Klingner, J, Boele, A., Linan-Thompson, S., & Rodriguez, D. (2014). *Essential components of special education for English language learners with learning disabilities.* DOI:10.1111/ldrp.12040

Kozleski, E. B. (2010) *Culturally responsive teaching matters. Equity Alliance.* Retrieved from http://files.eric.ed.gov/fulltext/ED520957.pdf

Hawkins, B.L., Cory, L.A., McGuire, F.A., & Allen, L.R. (2012). Therapeutic Recreation in education: Considerations for therapeutic Recreation practitioners, school systems, and policy makers. *Journal of Disability Policy Studies.* DOI:10.1177/1044207311418659

Lenihan, D., McCobb, E., Diurba, A., Linder, D., & Freeman, L. (2016). Measuring the effects of reading assistance dogs on reading ability and attitudes in elementary school children. *Journal of Research in Childhood Education: JRCE Association for Childhood Education International,* 30(2), 252–259. Retrieved from https://www.ncbi.nlm.nih.gov/pmc/articles/PMC4868357/

le Roux, M. C., Swartz, L., & Swart, E. (2014). The Effect of an Animal-Assisted Reading Program on the Reading Rate, Accuracy and Comprehension of Grade 3 Students: A Randomized Control. Child Youth Care Forum (43), 655–673. Retrieved from www.researchgate.net/profile/Marieanna_Le_Roux/publication/288519301

Lo, L. (2012). Demystifying the IEP process for diverse parents of children with disabilities. Retrieved from http://olms.cte.jhu.edu/olms2/data/ck/sites/271/files/Week03_Lo.pdf

Martins, A.J., Cumming, T.M., O'Neill, S.C., & Strnadová, I. (2017). Social and emotional competence and at-risk children's wellbeing: The roles of personal and interpersonal agency for children with ADHD, emotional and behavioral disorder, learning disability, and developmental disability. In E. Frydenberg., A.J. Martin., & R.J. Collie (Eds). *Social and emotional learning in Australia and the Asia Pacific.* Singapore: Springer.

McFerran, K., & Rickson, D. (2014) Community music therapy in schools: Realigning with the needs of contemporary students, staff and systems. *International Journal of Community Music,* 7(1), Retrieved from https://www.researchgate.net/profile/Katrina_Mcferran/publication/262775418

McFerran, K.S., & Shoemark. (2013). How musical engagement promotes well-being in education contexts: The case of a young man with profound and multiple disabilities. *International Journal of Qualitative Studies on Health and Well-being.* 8(1), 88-102. Retrieved from https://www.ncbi.nlm.nih.gov/pubmed/23930986

Mead, A.E. (2017). *Understanding parents school experiences and how it influences their intent to engage with their child's school.* (Unpublished dissertation). Northeastern University. Boston, MA.

Merritt, E. G., Wanless, S. B., Rimm-Kaufman, S. E., & Peugh, J. L. (2012). The contribution of teachers' emotional support to children's social behaviors and self-regulatory skills in first grade. *School Psychology Review*, 41(2), 141–159. Retrieved from https://eric.ed.gov/?id=EJ977431

More, Hart & Cheatham, G.A. (2013). *Language interpretation for diverse families: Considerations for special education teachers.* DOI: 10.1177/1053451212472229

Morena, G. & Gaytan, F. (2012). Reducing subjectivity in special education referrals by educators working with Latino students: using functional behavioral assessment as a prereferral practice in student support teams. *Emotional and Behavioral Difficulties*, 1–14. Retrieved from https://eric.ed.gov/?id=EJ1010796

Office of Disease Prevention and Health Promotion. (2016). *Health related quality of life and well-being.* Retrieved from https://www.healthypeople.gov/2020/topicsobjectives/topic/healthrelated-quality-of-life-well-being.

Olivos, E. M., Gallagher, R. J., & Aguilar, J. (2010). Fostering collaboration with culturally and linguistically diverse families of children with moderate to severe disabilities. *Journal of Educational & Psychological Consultation*, 20(1), 28-40. Retrieved from https://eric.ed.gov/?id=EJ879672

Quinton, S. (2013). *Good teachers embrace their students' cultural backgrounds.* Retrieved from https://www.theatlantic.com/education/archive/2013/11/good-teachers-embrace-their-students-cultural-backgrounds/281337/

Raty, H. (2011). Past in the present: the way parents remember their own school years relates to the way they participate in their child's schooling and remember his/her school years. *Social Psychology of Education*, 14, 347-360. doi.org/10.1007/s11218-010-9149-4

Response to Intervention Network. (n.d.). *Working with culturally and linguistically diverse families.* Retrieved from http://www.rtinetwork.org/learn/diversity/culturalcompetence

Ruiz, M.I. (2012). Factors that influence the participation of immigrant Latino parents in the special education process of their children with disabilities. Retrieved from http://scholarworks.uno.edu/cgi/viewcontent.cgi?article=2597&context=td

Sanchez, S. (2017). Social-emotional learning as a pathway for student well-being, confidence and success. *Academy for Social-Emotional Learning in Schools.* Retrieved from http://sel.cse.edu.social-emotional-learning-as-a-pathway-to-student-well-beingconfidence-and-success/

Schweizer, C., Knorth, E., & Spreen, S. (2014) Art therapy with children with Autism Spectrum Disorders: A review of clinical case descriptions on 'what works'. *The Arts in Psychotherapy.* http://dx.doi.org/10.1016/j.aip.2014.10.009.

Suárez-Orozco, C., Yoshikawa, H., Teranishi, T., & Suárez-Orozco. M. (2011). Living in the Shadows: The developmental implications of undocumented status [Special Issue].

Harvard Education Review, 81, 438-472. Retrieved from http://oppenheimer.mcgill.ca/IMG/pdf/Growing_up.pdf

Telzer, E. H., Gonzales, N. & Fuligni, A. J. (2014). Family obligation values and family assistance behaviors: Protective and risk factors for Mexican-American Adolescents' Substance Abuse. *Journal of Youth Adolescents*, 43(2), 270-283, doi:10.1007/s10964013-9941-5.

Villegas-Gutierrez, M. (2015). *Special education assessment process for culturally and linguistically diverse (CLD) students: 2015 update*. Retrieved from http://5c2cabd466efc6790a0a-6728e7c952118b70f16620a9fc754159.r37.cf1.rackcdn.com/cms/Special_Education_Assessment_Process_for_Culturally_and_Liguistically_Diverse_%28CLD%29_Students_with_logos_and_links_1489.pdf

Wells, A.M., Fox, L. & Cordova-Cobo, D., (2016). *How racially diverse schools and classrooms can benefit all students.* Retrieved from https://tcf.org/content/report/how-racially-diverse-schools-and-classrooms-can-benefit-all-students/

Wylie, C. & Bonne, L. (2015). *Secondary Schools in 2015: Findings from the NZCER National Survey.* Retrieved from http://www.nzcer.org.nz/research/publications/secondary-schools-2015

Chapter 10

Navigating New Turning Points: Transitioning Students with Learning Disabilities to Post-Secondary Promise

Christine N. Michael and
Nicholas D. Young, *American International College*

When thinking about a student's transition to post-secondary education, primary emphasis is usually placed on academic preparation. This is particularly true for students with learning disabilities, as parents, teachers, guidance counselors and students go about selecting an appropriate college, academic major, career path, and support services. Because so many students with learning disabilities may have experienced difficulties with classroom skills, and with auxiliary academic functions such as organization, time management, note taking or testing, it seems essential to emphasize strategies for academic success.

Preparation for college in the socio-emotional sphere, however, may be even more important. Stress, isolation, finding an affinity group, navigating family issues, and becoming an advocate for oneself all are among the top reasons for students leaving college without a degree; these variables are even more difficult for marginalized groups, such as first-generation, low-income, minority, or students with learning disabilities. The national average for students completing their four-year degree within six years is 59%, yet only 27% of students who have disclosed their disabilities do so (Institute of Educational Sciences, 2011 National Longitudinal Transition Study-2).

Typically, college students who have learning disabilities suffer lower rates of retention and degree completion rates when compared to their non-disabled peers; it also takes them longer to earn their degrees (Murray, Goldstein, Nourse, & Edgar, 2000; Wessel,

Jones, Markle, & Westfall, 2009). Murray et al. in their five-year follow-up of 1990 graduates and ten-year follow-up of 1985 graduates, reported that only 19% of students with disabilities had graduated after five years, and 43 % at ten. When looking only at four-year college completion, a scant 2.4% of Students with learning disabilities had graduated at ten years, compared to 45% of their non-disabled peers. A host of factors—most of them non-academic—influences this sad statistic.

Theories and research on college retention and student success are grounded in the sociological model and formulated on the notion that students are primarily social beings whose interactions with the broader social structure on campus is key to a positive campus experience and academic success. In the 1970s, Astin and Tinto identified the socio-emotional realm of college experience as the most critical aspect of retention to graduation, as well as a student's citizenship on the campus and beyond. Astin (1984) articulated the concept of involvement: students who were more involved, and thus more likely to succeed, invested their time and energy in numerous relationships—with faculty, other students, clubs, teams and organizations, volunteer and leadership relationships, and those in the larger community. The quality of relationships, represented by the degree of his or her investment, is the main determinant of the student's desire to remain engaged with the college community.

Tinto's work (1993) was founded on the concept that the more academically and socially involved a student becomes, the more s/he makes a commitment to the institution and to persisting to graduation. Social commitment, Tinto wrote, becomes academic commitment. His theories have been called "interactionalist" and "theory of integration," but regardless of label, they clearly demonstrate the primacy of social networks in determining retention.

Spady (1970) concurred with Tinto (1993), saying that students who form relationships with faculty, staff and peers, share the values of the college and community, or have meaningful connections to others are far more likely to be retained to graduation. He created a model that contains five independent variables that influence student persistence; grade performance and intellectual development are the only two that do not fall into the social domain. Normative congruence—a sense of fitting in with the social norms and values of one's peers—in addition to friendship support and the umbrella factor of "social integration" are the variables that indicate how powerful the social domain is in influencing post-secondary success.

Most of scholarly literature and research on the transition to college centers on academic readiness and the cognitive domain. While these obviously are critical topics, one also must consider the roles of the psychological and social domains. The ACT study (2004) of college retention found that ACT scores and high school grade points were far less important than social support and involvement when measuring successful college retention. Many students who had performed poorly in secondary school persisted to college graduation because they were socially integrated and felt themselves to be a vital part of the college campus. This feeling of social integration is extremely critical for students who come from marginalized populations, including Students with learning disabilities. The ACT study highlighted the fact that one of the key variables influencing college retention is that each student has what s/he describes as a quality relationship with at least one person on campus.

Knowing these facts, it is the responsibility of secondary teachers, staff, parents, and Students with learning disabilities themselves to round out their transition preparation with greater attention to the socio-emotional factors that can bolster their chances for success.

Developmental Tasks That Take Place During the Emerging Adult Transition

The transition from adolescence to emerging adulthood is filled with critical developmental tasks that the adolescent and emerging adult must master successfully. Seminal scholarly literature describes a set of common tasks for the adolescent-to-emerging adult transition (Kuther, 2016; Arnett, 2015; Laursen & Collins, 2012; Shek & Wong, 2011; Gentry & Campbell, 2002).

In recent years, Arnett (2015) coined a new phrase, "emerging adulthood," to describe the developmental stage from age 18-25. He felt the necessity of doing this because of the longer road to adulthood that American youth are taking. Not adulthood, and not adolescence, this stage is comprised of five features: identity explorations; instability; self-focus; feeling in between; and possibility/optimism.

Arnett's (2015) work brings a sharper focus to the socioemotional tasks of emerging adulthood. For example, when discussing identity explorations, he notes that during this period, "neither beholden to their parents, nor committed to an assortment of adult roles, they have an exceptional opportunity to try out different ways of living and different possible choices for love and work" (p.9). However, as one can imagine, this greater freedom and wealth of possibilities can be experienced as overwhelming by Students with learning disabilities who may have had their previous decision making very much determined by others.

Arnett (2015) also speaks about this as a time of "instability" in which emerging adults know that they are supposed to have a Plan. But this Plan, which entails components of education, career, relationships, and residences, is frequently subject to modification given the feedback they receive as they try it out in "real life." For Students with learning disabilities who have not been active participants in developing their IEPs and ITPs, as well as other life choices, formulating a realistic Plan and being able to modify it as necessary may be an even more daunting task.

"Self-focus" is a descriptor that Arnett uses, not in a pejorative way, to describe the period of emerging adulthood. He notes that adolescents typically get to be more independent than they were in their childhood, but that parents, school, teachers, and other adults "set standards and monitor their behavior and performance" (2015, p.13). This is even more the case for the majority of Students with learning disabilities. The goal of self-focus, he writes, is for emerging adults to learn who they are, what they want, and what is necessary to build a foundation to reach those goals.

Those involved in Students with learning disabilities' transition planning need to provide activities that move them towards greater independence so that they are prepared for that independence when they move to post-secondary lives. Without such preparation, they are on a path to be emotionally overwhelmed by the tasks of the transition.

A feeling of being "in between" is how the participants in Arnett's interviews described this period of their lives. As they described them, the criteria for becoming an adult were to accept responsibility for oneself, make independent decisions, and become independent financially. Incremental steps needed to be taken towards meeting each of these criteria. With awareness that most Students with learning disabilities have had fewer opportunities than their non-disabled peers to do these things, it becomes incumbent on transition planners to focus on manageable steps towards this greater independence before post-secondary launching.

As one's identity becomes clearer, it is time to consider a choice of an initial career path; for college-bound adolescents, this step entails thinking about academic concentrations or majors. For those entering training programs or the world of work, decisions about preparation for careers that are good fits for the student's learning profile take on urgency. The tentative career plan gives the adolescent a sense of self-in-the-adult-world and helps to build greater feelings of confidence and efficacy.

Arnett (2015) also describes the emotional state of possibility/optimism as a primary characteristic of emerging adulthood. He sees it as a time of great optimism and high hopes, where young people believe that things can dramatically alter their life path after secondary school. It is a time for transforming oneself. While this is an exciting time full of future-oriented dreams, it also can be crushing if individuals are not capable of transforming or of fulfilling these dreams. Since many Students with learning disabilities may have a difficult time with setting realistic goals for themselves, or goals that are a good fit for their strengths and interests, they are at higher risk for potential failure or underachievement without attention to these issues prior to transition.

Identity is an extremely complex concept, in that it incorporates other variables such as race, ethnicity, and gender identity formation. The goal in identity consolidation at this time in life is to begin to pull together the various threads of one's identity and weave them into a coherent self that is stable over time (Kuther, 2016). Students who must grapple with multiple identities that put them at risk of marginalization (for example, LD and of color, or LD and first-generation) have more difficult work than mainstream students.

Beyond the five main features of this stage, there are other navigations that Arnett sees as pivotal. One is the difficult task of renegotiating roles with family. He speaks to moving from "conflict to companionship" as work of this period. Grigal and Hart (2010) point out that while secondary students who have received services learn valuable life skills, they usually do so in nurturing environments with a great deal of "hand-holding, security, and protection" (p.208).

Parents of Students with learning disabilities may feel that they must take on additional roles in order to ensure their child's success.

Shaw, Madaus, & Dukes III (2010) provide descriptions of such parents: the "agent," who intervenes in events such as career fairs, college visits, or administrative actions; the "white knight," who is an interventionist to "save the day" if problems arise; and the "black hawk," who takes unethical steps such as writing a paper or college essay to increase a student's chances of success (p. 154). While it is generally accepted that parents' involvement in schools decreases as children move from elementary to middle to secondary school, in the case of Students with learning disabilities' parents, the opposite often takes place.

While it is admirable that parents of students with disabilities want to assure their children's success during the transition, they must learn to balance their desire to ensure that success through their own efforts with providing the space that their children need to develop the self-advocacy and self-reliance tools that they need for college and beyond; attaining this greater degree of autonomy is complicated if parents cannot "cut the cord" to a healthy degree.

Arnett (2015) also explored the topic of intimacy—love and sex— with his informants. He discovered a landscape fraught with difficulties, from meeting potential partners to the "hook up culture," in which casual sex, often alcohol or drug-fueled, is more the norm. Given some of the deficits that Students with learning disabilities have in the socioemotional sphere, ranging from the inability to read social cues and body language, to underestimating risky situations, this task may be more complicated.

This also is a time to experiment with gender roles and form a tentative acceptance of one's own definition of male or female identity. New sexual feelings may lead to a false sense of intimacy with others. There also are issues with accepting one's body and body image.

Emerging adults need to find relationships beyond possible sexual partners—friendships, mentors, affinity groups, and the likes. Erikson (1994) noted that without intimate relationships, a young person is unable to complete the developmental task at hand and risks being isolated. Isolation can lead to depression, low self-esteem, or a lack of a sense of belonging, which Tinto (1993) and others found correlated positively with leaving college.

Mental Health and Emotional Well-being

There are mental health issues, as well. Adolescents with learning disabilities reportedly experience severe emotional distress at rates two to three times that of other adolescents; girls experience more emotional distress than boys. LD adolescents are more likely to have undergone emotional distress, suicidal thoughts or attempts or acts of violence. Having meaningful relationships, positive school experiences, and a faith community or spiritual belief in something larger than the self are factors that may lessen emotional problems in these categories, making emerging adults more resilient (Gentry & Campbell, 2002).

A significant benefit of post-secondary attendance is the opportunity to diversify one's social community, because college campuses embrace such a wide variety of students from different backgrounds, cultures and beliefs. But, "statistics show that high school graduates with disabilities report a high level of social isolation once they exit school and usually participate in activities meant only for other people with disabilities." Tragically, this is just the opposite of what occurs for the non-disabled college population (Grigal & Hart, 2010, p. 201).

Smith (2011) sees that substance abuse in this age demographic as an attempt to locate happiness and make social connections. However, for the emerging adults he interviewed for his research, this activity led them to a "fake feeling of happiness" (p.110). While some described the activity from the standpoint of meeting new people, others spoke of "stress, blues, and boredom" (p.118). Other researchers stress several key tasks that attend this stage of development.

Developing a Moral Compass

In the absence of one's parents and community of origin, the emerging adult must learn to make ethical decisions using his or her own moral compass. Sometimes, this involves reliance on values from family or community of origin, or important institutions such as one's faith community or school. But post-secondary education is bound to bring many of these values under greater scrutiny, as well as expose the young person to values systems that may be wildly different from those s/he holds. Eventually, the emerging adult comes to a more authentic values system to help him or her face increasingly complex ethical and moral situations.

Smith (2011), in his fascinating book *Lost in Transition*, speaks of "morality adrift" after interviewing 18-23-year-olds and notes that while most emerging adults are not morally bankrupt, they are "lost." He writes: "They do not adequately know the moral landscape of the real world they inhabit...They need some better moral maps and better-equipped guides to show them the way around. The question is, do those maps and guides exist, and can they be put to use?" (p.69).

Social Integration and Acceptance

Post-secondary experiences, for the most part, expose emerging adults to new social roles, greater diversity in social contacts, and more independence. Although it was noted earlier that this is less true for students with disabilities, this transition still presents difficult developmental work, as it can require the young person to question previously unexamined roles passed down from his or her family, culture, and community of origin and experiment with novel constructions of the self. This can result in feelings of confusion, disloyalty, or being torn between disparate "worlds."

Students from marginalized groups also may feel that they are "imposters" on campus and may undergo emotions of anxiety of being "found out" or a sense of unworthiness, regardless of whether they are succeeding on campus or not (Davis, 2010). Social connections and identities may emerge from memberships in teams, affinity groups, clubs, or organizations, and from community-based activities such as internships, work experiences, or mentorship and can serve as buffers to emotional challenges in acclimation.

Challenges to Socioemotional Development During Adolescence for Students with Learning Disabilities

While not all students struggle in the socio-emotional domain, most have some issues to address, and the best time to do so is during the transition, rather than in the hectic and turbulent first days of college. Preparation by the LD student and his or her transition team plays a primary role in socioemotional success, and the transition plan can be invaluable in laying out specifics of that preparation.

There are wide-ranging estimates of incidence of social problems in Students with learning disabilities; these range anywhere from 38% to 75% of the identified population (Bryan, Burstein, & Ergul, 2004) and appear across all demographic variables. In the authors' review of science-based research on the social skills of students with LD, they consistently found deficits in self-concept, greater feelings of loneliness, problems with social information processing, social cognition and communicative competence, and lack of skills in initiating and sustaining positive social relationships. Not all students with learning disabilities possessed these characteristics, but those who did struggled with many of the subtle skills integral to forming friendships and social networks.

Students with learning disabilities also may not be as adept at extracting information from the social environment that may be critical to successful adaptation to a classroom or community. Without well-honed abilities to read social cues, gain information from one's environment, appreciate humor or idiosyncrasies of communication, read body language or initiate conversations, the LD student may be barred from the fullest participation in social situations (Bryan, Burstein, & Ergul, 2004).

Elias (2004) identified the fifteen key skills that make up "emotional intelligence." These include: recognizing one's own and others' emotions; regulating and managing strong emotions; recognizing one's strengths and areas for growth; listening and communicating accurately and clearly; being able to take another's perspective and sense his/her emotions; respecting others and self and appreciating differences; correctly identifying problems; setting goals that are positive and realistic; problem solving, decision making and planning; approaching others and building positive relationships; resisting negative peer pressure; cooperating, negotiating and managing conflicts; working effectively in groups; seeking and giving help; and showing ethical and social responsibility (p. 54).

Elias (2004) believes that all involved in transition planning must help Students with learning disabilities learn these skills and have opportunities to practice them over time. This is critical to the post-secondary transition, as well, because each of the key skills is integrally linked to success on the college campus. These skills are bound to forming relationships with faculty and peers, seeking help when needed, making healthy personal choices, negotiating classroom and dorm life, and becoming a positive member of the learning community. Gorman (1999) stresses the necessity of teaching skills to develop resiliency and emotional well-being, since emotions and education go hand in hand.

Socioemotional Issues Students with learning disabilities Face During the Transition to Post-Secondary Education

For all students, the challenges of transitioning from high school to post-secondary are daunting, as they must make progress in forming a more unique identity, become more autonomous, and separate emotionally and usually geographically from parents and community of origin. This is a difficult enough set of tasks, but as Larose et al. (2005) note, emerging adults do not have the luxury of working solely on these psychosocial tasks. They also must rapidly adjust to a new set of academic, social and emotional demands made by their new college culture. For Students with learning disabilities, there are even more steps to the transition.

Acceptance of One's Disability

Statistics garnered from the 2014 study, The State of Learning Disabilities (Cortiella & Horowitz) show a radical shift in secondary students' acceptance of the LD label once they graduate from high school. According to (Cortiella & Horowitz, 2014), within two years of leaving high school, 52% of identified Students with learning disabilities no longer identified themselves to have a disability; within eight years of leaving, that number had ballooned to 68%. Students do not make post-secondary officials aware of their disability. Only 24% of graduates informed post-secondary institutions of their disabilities, yet 44% of Students with learning disabilities who never received help in college later reflected that they believed that some would have been helpful (Cortiella & Horowitz, 2014). College personnel cite lack of disclosure of disabilities as a major reason for the low graduation rate among Students with learning disabilities and note that more needs to be done to make Students with learning disabilities, their families and their transition team more aware of the implications of not disclosing at the college level.

Eye-to-Eye is a national organization specifically working with Students with learning disabilities. Goldfus (2015) surveyed Eye-To-Eye student coordinators around the country to discover what strategies they view as integral to campus success for Students with learning disabilities, especially during the transition to campus. They overwhelmingly noted the importance of:

- Own your own LD; be proud to be a unique learner and embrace learning differences. For a variety of reasons, too many students hope to leave their disability behind when they leave high school, but if they accept and embrace their own unique learning profile, they will be more successful.
- Use services that are provided
- Be well versed in your learning style, learning needs, and how to articulate your needs

- Communicate with professors
- Know what resources are present beyond the Office of Disability Services
- Don't view asking for help as a weakness
- Don't feel isolated, but reach out to a larger community of LD learners, network even before you arrive on campus
- Get out of your academic comfort zone and explore different courses that draw your interests
- Become an advocate for oneself

At the K-12 level, the responsibility for identifying, monitoring, and providing support for each LD student belongs to his or her school or school district. This radically shifts to the student's responsibility once s/he enters the post-secondary world. As Goldberg notes, "in college, students are usually on their own making their educational choices. However, if students do not understand their disability and have not practiced asking for recommended accommodations, they will have a hard time accessing needed services" (p.2).

Some students may not even be aware that they now must self-identify or provide documentation of their disability in order to receive accommodative services. No one else will perform these services for them, and if parents call trying to intervene, they will be told to have the student him or herself make the contact (Goldberg, 2017).

Untethering from Familiar Supports

Hadley (2007) conducted qualitative research to better understand, from the perspective of students with learning disabilities, how they navigated the transition to college and what role accommodations played. Citing three of Chickering's (1969) vectors of competence, she found that "managing emotions" was fraught with challenges. "The students seemed exceptionally dependent upon the services they had grown accustomed to in high school" (p.12). They had difficulty imagining success without those services, particularly since there was so much individualized attention to their needs. In order to achieve greater autonomy, students needed help in moving from the familiarity of the personalized services of their secondary school experiences to the supports provided on their college campuses.

Finding Emotional Connectedness Through Affinity Groups

One of the keys to student retention is that a student finds emotional connectedness and meaning through belonging to at least one group. These "affinity groups" may be clubs, sports teams, volunteer groups, leadership organizations, or individuals who are formed into associations through some commonality such as being a member living/learning dorm community or an advisee group. Groups like the latter are randomly formed without the student's participation, but others entail seeking out membership, and perhaps even auditioning or applying to become a member.

Some group membership is not necessarily desirable, such as being part of a support group for students with LD or being recommended to the tutorial or counseling center. Initially finding affinity groups that have meaning for Students with learning disabilities also may require a more difficult process because of social skills, language, or other deficits.

Career exploration and service learning courses can be extremely valuable opportunities for helping students find peers and mentors with similar interests and backgrounds. The curriculum itself may help students with social networking, since there are far more opportunities in college to take classes of interest than are available in most high schools. In such major, elective and field-based courses, Students with learning disabilities make natural connections and informal networking may occur, diversifying their peer contacts.

Developing Self-Understanding and Self-Assessment Skills

Students with disabilities are assessed academically throughout their K-12 experience, but assessment aimed at post-secondary success needs to include all the domains necessary to thrive on campus. Shaw, Madau, & Dukes (2010) maintain that the following are skills integral to college success: self-determination and self-advocacy skills; understanding rights and responsibilities; study, note-taking, and time management skills; reading, math, and writing ability; and social skills and recreational activities.

Self-understanding, Goldberg writes, is the key to success: "Students who understand the reasons they do well in some activities and the reasons they struggle with others take the first step in working through challenging situations. Preferably students should come to this understanding before they are faced with exams or papers in their first college courses" (p.2). The same can be said for socioemotional activities.

Students with learning disabilities have undergone myriad assessments by the time they graduate high school, but the essential shift in transitional assessment is that they now are responsible for self-assessment. On the college campus, all students partake in acts of self-assessment on a regular basis: in choosing courses and majors; in finding internship and work settings with a good fit; in finding social niches and affinity groups; in making wise decisions about issues such as sexual activity, risk taking, and substance abuse; and in monitoring their choices to ensure that there is congruence between those choices and actions and the goals they have set for themselves.

Awareness of Mental Health Issues

Shek and Wong (2011) highlight the fact that adolescence is a time of rapid developmental change in all domains and that issues arising in adolescence typically do not abate or disappear immediately when one transitions to post-secondary settings. In fact, issues may be exacerbated in many cases, as students undergo a battery of changes. Transition planning for Students with learning disabilities entails addressing common mental health challenges on college campuses, as well as particular risks for each LD student head on.

Successful persistence to graduation, the authors note, requires withstanding a bombardment of stressors. This theme is replayed in Kadison and DiGermonimo's book, *College of the Overwhelmed* (2005). Inextricably linked to the complex issue of cultivating positive emotional health and approaches to dealing with risk-taking, depression, loneliness, sexuality, substance abuse, and other problems salient on college campuses are the individualized stressors related to each LD student's profile and background.

One major function of transition planning must be anticipatory education aimed at providing Students with learning disabilities with multiple opportunities to problem solve and rehearse responses to situations they may encounter. Students with learning disabilities need to be aware of their own "triggers", be able to employ methods to build their own physical, emotional and spiritual health, and know sources of support on the college campus before they enroll formally. They also need to recognize how they have been resilient in prior challenges so that they can draw on these strategies and stances in future situations. With this kind of preparation, they are more resilient when encountering socioemotional challenges. Knowing that everyone else on campus, especially freshmen, faces socioemotional challenges can normalize the discussion.

While authors such as Shek and Wong (2011) urge colleges to offer credit-bearing courses on topics of physical and emotional health and well-being, it is the rare institution that goes beyond paying lip service to holistic development in young people. Thus, it is critical that transition planning over the secondary years assumes primary responsibility for providing such a curriculum, whether formal, informal, or a combination of both. Otherwise, students with LD will enter the post-secondary arena underprepared to succeed in the socioemotional sphere.

Strategies for Successfully Navigating the Emerging Adult Transition

Socioemotional development and skills are essential to a successful transition to college; therefore, a plethora of strategies can and should be employed. These include mentoring, networking, direct teaching of self-advocacy skills, learning to self-assess, intentional instruction in social skills, positive parental involvement, campus based programs before matriculation, and taking a holistic approach to transition planning.

Mentoring

Mentoring is perhaps the most powerful socio-emotional tool for the transition to college—for students with or without learning disabilities. Pairing Students with learning disabilities with more advanced students with LD can be invaluable. The mentor can answer questions honestly, provide strategies that worked for him or her, simulate case examples of situations that might be encountered on campus and help the secondary student rehearse for those scenarios, and assist the student in developing networks and relationships that can be in place prior to actual arrival on campus.

Formal mentoring programs can be set up with most colleges through their office of disabilities services; larger institutions have personnel who provide a variety of different kinds of mentoring: academic; sports; service organizations; or affinity groups. Schools also can set up mentoring experiences, in person or through e-mentoring, with their own alumni/ae who have LD. Inviting successful college students back to speak at their high schools or tapping them to be e-mentors are ways to highlight the success of students with learning disabilities. Organizations such as the National Institute of Justice run e-mentoring programs for Students with learning disabilities. And mentors also provide support for Students with learning disabilities labeled as "gifted" (Shevitz et al., 2003).

Nationwide, there are mentoring programs specifically for Students with learning disabilities. The program is based on techniques that mentors share with mentees: metacognitive skills; self-advocacy; and proactive learning strategies. Teachers College, Columbia University, conducted independent research and found that Students with learning disabilities reported improvement in self-esteem, positive role modeling, hope for the future, and self-advocacy.

Mentorship extends well into the socio-emotional domain, as mentors can fill a number of roles that are essential to college success, but that might not be recognized as being as critical as academic skills and support systems. These include nutrition, exercise, spiritual well-being, money management, transportation, safety, and the likes (Moore, 2015).

Networking

Each LD student, prior to graduation from high school, should have identified potential sources to tap at the post-secondary level prior to graduation. This network might involve college students from his or her high school who are attending the college of choice or e-networking/mentoring networks with peers who have chosen to attend other colleges. Adults who could serve as mentors can be located through having a sense of the clubs, organizations, or community groups (such as churches, volunteer organizations, or job sites) that have imbedded mentoring—formal and informal—into their missions; this allows for connections to be formed prior to actual arrival on campus.

Joining one of the national organizations dedicated to students with learning disabilities is another way to network. Membership helps to increase disability awareness and empowers the student to become an advocate for others; publications, conferences and trainings are offered regularly to members of these organizations, and students can build their confidence by upping their knowledge, meeting others who have been successful, and learning advocacy skills at the individual, local and national level. The Heath Resource

Directory (George Washington University) and the National Resources for Adults with Learning Disabilities are excellent sources of contact information and descriptions of the major national organizations.

Direct Teaching of Self-Advocacy Skills

Self-determination skills are a critical part of a successful postsecondary transition for students with LD, and thus must be made an intentional part of transitional planning. Self-determination training immerses the student in decision making, whom to include in decision-making processes, and self-advocacy tools that allow the student to assume control of his/her life. This process entails mastering the ability to articulate and advocate for needed services, supports, and experiences; unfortunately, students with disabilities are not often afforded opportunities to rehearse, let alone practice these skills enough times to refine and master them (Grigal & Hart, 2010).

Students with disabilities advocate best for themselves and other Students with learning disabilities, the Learning and Education about Disabilities (LEAD) Project found (LD Online, 2017). An innovative self-determination program permits Students with learning disabilities to take on the responsibility for their education and to become skillful advocates for themselves and others. LD high school students receive mentoring and weekly support sessions to teach them self-awareness techniques and impart knowledge about disabilities. Students learn both the accommodations that are available and that they need, and how to articulate those to teachers and others.

The students in LEAD programs also practice making presentations to parents and community groups. Serving as mentors to middle and elementary school students with learning disabilities, they gain a sense of power and esteem through being able to assist others. They also receive mentor training that prepares them to assume this role on a college campus. By using an assets-based approach, they learn to advocate from a position of strengths, rather than deficits.

Learning to Self-Assess

Understanding the nature of one's learning disabilities as well as individual strengths and weaknesses is one key to emotional and academic well-being. Using interest and career inventories, learning styles and multiple intelligences assessments, personal and cultural styles appraisals, and other assets-based approaches helps each student identify gifts and abilities s/he brings to a college setting. In the socioemotional and health realms, there are inventories to assess potential stressors and triggers, as well as aspects of resilience that the student has used or can use to overcome challenges.

Another resource is the Postsecondary Education Research Center (PERC) Self-Advocacy Checklist. The checklist helps the transition team identify the skills that need to be developed and current people with whom Students with learning disabilities can practice the skills. Self-knowledge also comes from exposure to many, diverse hobbies, activities and experiences, and people; these can help a young person figure out where s/he excels and what academic concentrations and career paths might be consonant with those strengths. It should be an articulated goal for each secondary LD student to be able to coherently describe his or her disabilities, interests, strengths and goals for the future prior to setting foot on the college campus.

Intentional Instruction in Social Skills

While the precise degree of a didactic approach to social skills is not clear, there appear to be some benefits to be considered in transition planning. Cook, Gresham, Kern, Barreras, Thornton, & Crews (2008) analyzed the meta-analytic literature on the use of social skills training with EBT students, and they reported that two-thirds of students with or at risk for EBT respond favorably to remediation interventions through the teaching of social skills. However, they also warn that secondary students with social skills deficits can expect to experience challenges in their post-secondary lives without greater attention and resources provided in this domain.

Valenti (2005) speaks of the psychological and emotional scars that Students with learning disabilities may have accumulated by the time they reach secondary school, due to academic and social failures. He recommends that every LD high school student's Individual Transition Plan includes clear goals for the achievement of the following psychosocial skills: problem-solving; goal-setting; time management; decision making; conflict resolution; improving self-concept; sensitivity training; making friends; exploring one's disability; anxiety reduction; job-searching skills; overcoming resentment; accepting criticism; and vocational decision making.

All skills are required for a successful transition, as poor social-judgment frequently leads to post-secondary educational, social and vocational failures. Transition team partners should vary methods to develop the skills and make them generalizable to multiple situations so that students can function autonomously. Valenti (2005) recommends using individual and group counseling, coaching and mentoring, career inventories and counseling, and using methods aligned to students' learning styles and multiple intelligences (films, lectures, readings, dramatizations) to build and augment the social skills needed for post-secondary success. Social skills education, he contends, is most effective when it is individualized to the greatest extent possible (Valenti, 2005).

Positive Parental Involvement

In their 2017 study, Lowe & Dotterer explored parental involvement during the college transition. Subscribing to Arnett's (2015) identification of emerging adulthood as a distinct developmental period, they set out to understand the role that parental involvement, both emotional and practical, played during the stage. They note Tanner's (2006) concept of "recentering," which is described as a process of replacing other-regulated behavior with self-regulated behavior. Recentering takes place in three phases, with shifts from seeking out contexts that support autonomy (such as college) to fully assuming adult roles that complete self-sufficiency.

As Arnett (2015) noted, parents continue to play key roles during emerging adulthood, but Lowe & Dotterer wanted to discover what roles best support the attainment of autonomy and self-sufficiency in their children. They review three key components: parental support-giving; parent-student contact; and parental academic engagement. In terms of student outcomes, provision of emotional support was positively linked to academic outcomes, including GPA and retention. They found that high levels of support and communication with parents led to lower levels of depression, loneliness, and risk-taking.

Lowe & Dotterer (2017) also found that freshmen whose parents frequently made contact with college officials to intervene on their children's behalf had lower academic achievement, as did high levels of parental financial support. Over-involvement on the part of student-athletes' parents appeared to hinder students' development of autonomy.

These findings are important in discussions with the parents of Students with learning disabilities, as they typically have had a higher degree of involvement in their children's education than parents of non-disabled peers. Transition planning must take into account the best ways to support Students with learning disabilities, but also recognize strategies for promoting steps towards autonomy and self-sufficiency.

Families—however they may be defined and configured—must play a vital role in helping the LD student during the college transition. However, this entails a delicate balancing act, as family members must be supportive, yet also accept and encourage opportunities for greater autonomy. Roffman (2007) urges parents to be actively involved in, and to engage their children as fully in possible in leading, the transition planning process. She also reminds them to hold flexible attitudes and employ open-minded listening when considering all alternatives in transitional planning. Her book, *Guiding Teens with Learning Disabilities: Navigating the Transition from High School to Adulthood*, includes reflective activities that parents can use in preparation for transition planning meetings.

Family can best accomplish this goal by: being involved in transition planning activities and including the student; helping him or her develop realistic goals; encouraging realistic post-secondary options; communicating confidence in the student's ability to be successful; and encouraging the student to develop maximal independence in all aspects of life in preparation for success in post-secondary settings.

For parents who may not have attended college themselves, there also is a steep learning curve that must be handled respectfully by school officials. Family members should be kept abreast of all social skills training and "college knowledge" sessions so that they can reinforce necessary skills and attitudes at home; they should be viewed as potential coaches for their children in the psychosocial realm and must recognize and embrace the changing developmental relationship as their children transition to young adulthood.

Roffman (2007) believes that many parents need information and support in considering socioemotional and mental health challenges that may present themselves after graduation. Addressing these as part of transition planning, by assessing issues such as depression, anxiety, impulsivity, and inability to read social cues can provide students with didactic interventions in school and teach parents strategies to bolster prosocial behaviors at home.

Campus-Based Programs Before Matriculation

One of the best preparations for successful transition—for all students—is to get secondary students on college campuses prior to their actual matriculation. This is incredibly useful for Students with learning disabilities, as they need exposure in order become familiar with the "nuts and bolts" of how a campus operates, what resources they can access and where they are located, and what the social "norms" of the college community are. Attending a college summer program is helpful, and being able to attend a program on the actual campus to which one will matriculate is even more meaningful.

Lasting anywhere from a few days to a month, these programs most commonly are offered to rising high school seniors or those just graduated. Each spring, the HEATH Resource Center at the National Youth Transitions Center (George Washington University) publishes a list of Summer Pre-College Programs for Students with Learning Disabilities. Dual-enrollment situations in which secondary students can take college courses also familiarize them with expectations and flow of college-level classes, although there is little emphasis on the socio-emotional aspects of college life.

Students with learning disabilities transitioning to college also might consider the three-week "boot camps" run by Landmark College, which specializes in educating Students with learning disabilities, or the residential programs run by the non-profit College Internship Program (Marklein, 2011). These programs intentionally teach many of the "soft" skills vital to college success.

Taking a Holistic Approach to Transition Planning

Since most college campuses do not yet see it as their responsibility to provide credit-bearing courses, or curriculum to help students with learning disabilities integrate successfully and maintain academic and socioemotional well-being, those responsible for transition planning for Students with learning disabilities at the secondary level must fill this void. Shek and Wong (2011) identified fourteen youth assets that must be created and supported in adolescents and emerging adults; examples include developing social, behavioral, emotional, cognitive and moral competence and resilience.

Mentoring, community and school involvement, and collaboration with families are integral aspects of preparation for the transition. Direct teaching of social skills, promoting opportunities for prosocial involvement in school and community, and building student confidence through the setting of meaningful future goals and the steps to achieve those goals again should be part of all secondary education and transition planning. Likewise, teaching and modeling the prosocial norms necessary for classroom participation, dorm living, and other social milieus can be accomplished both in transition planning and in campus-based orientation and summer programs.

Developing self-efficacy and self-determination skills has been mentioned previously, so one can see that Shek and Wong's model parallels closely good transition planning prior to the college experience. Shek & Wong (2011) emphasize building resilience in students through bolstering their capacity to withstand change and stressful events; knowing one's stressors, stress reduction and stress management all are inextricably linked to resilience. Some creative new approaches include the incorporation of meditation, mindfulness and activities such as yoga into school-based routines.

These activities are prevalent on college campuses and help to mitigate stress, isolation, and anxiety and promote general affective well-being (Davis & Hayes, 2012; Keng, Smoski, & Robins, 2011). Discussing one's spiritual life, however that is defined, and identifying sources of meaning and purpose that might exist in a college campus and curriculum help secondary students see possible activities, academics, and affinity groups to support them when they transition. Creating a transition checklist, based on the aforementioned skills and experiences, makes tangible the areas to be mastered prior to graduation. Where, how and with whom these skills are to be developed in conjunction with each student and his/her transition team should be articulated clearly.

Conclusion

It is not enough to increase college access for students with learning disabilities; despite the increasing numbers of Students with learning disabilities transitioning to two and four-year colleges, there is much more work to be done. Being accepted to college, but failing to graduate, can be devastating to Students with learning disabilities and their families—emotionally, financially, and career-wise. Students with learning disabilities and their transition teams must consider that path to success on campus traverses multiple, intertwined domains, not the least of which is the psychosocial realm, blending social, emotional, relational and spiritual development.

Due to the abundance of attention paid to academic preparation, Students with learning disabilities too frequently are deficient in the socioemotional skills necessary for post-secondary success. Transition teams must extend their work in the cognitive and academic realms with direct modeling, mentoring and instruction in other skills equally important for success. As research by Tinto, Bean, and others has shown, even academically well-prepared students can fail to persist and thrive if they cannot fully join the life of the college campus, develop social networks, and find personal meaning in their college campus experiences; conversely, students with less than stellar academic skills may persist to graduation due to their feelings of belonging to the college and its constituent groups.

Students with learning disabilities may be at even greater risk for health and mental health challenges once on the college campus. Discussion and strategizing for maintaining optimal health and resiliency need to take place during post-secondary and transition times. Families need to be educated in how to help students' transitions progress smoothly and how to help their students during the critical first year of college. IEPs and ITPs must extend beyond their articulated academic and post-secondary career goals to include goals and strategies for maximizing assets that lead the LD student to a well-rounded, satisfying life during his or her college years, and well beyond.

Points to Remember

- *Socioemotional factors are equally or potentially even more important than academic preparation in post-secondary success.*

- *Many students with learning disabilities face challenges and deficits in their socio-emotional development; therefore, these skills should be assessed early in their secondary education and specific strategies for strengthening areas of weakness and noting areas of strength should be articulated.*

- *The parents of students with learning disabilities frequently have been very involved in their children's education; thus, they need direct knowledge and coaching in how to navigate the young adult transition in a way that both supports their children, yet allows them the space to develop greater autonomy and independence.*

- *Mentors, positive adult role models, successful college students with learning disabilities, and school and college organizations can serve powerful roles in prosocial development.*

- *Students with learning disabilities may be at even higher risk for physical and mental health issues on college campuses, and so secondary students with LD should be educated about ways to maintain cognitive, physical, emotional and spiritual health through approaches such as being aware of resources, building their own resiliency, stress management and mindfulness, and seeking out positive and activities.*

References

ACT (2004). *What works in student retention.* Retrieved from www.act.org/research/policymakers/reports/retain.html.

Arnett, J.J. (2015). *Emerging adulthood.* New York, NY: Oxford University Press.

Astin, (1984). Student involvement: A developmental theory for higher education. *Journal of College Student Development,* 40, 518-529. Retrieved from https://eric.ed.gov/?id=EJ309521

Bryan,T., Burstein, K., & Ergul, C. (2004). The social-emotional side of learning disabilities: A science-based presentation of the state of the art. *Learning Disability Quarterly,* v27, 45-51. DOI:10.2307/1593631

Chickering, A.W. (1969). *Education and identity.* San Francisco, CA: Jossey-Bass.

Cook, C., Gresham, F., Kern, L., Barreras, R., Thornton, S., & Crews, S. (2008). Social skills training for secondary students with emotional and/or behavioral disorders. *Journal of Emotional and Behavioral Disorders,* v.16(3), 131-144. DOI:10.1177/1063426608314541

Cortiella, C & Horowitz, S. H. (2014). *The state of learning disabilities: Facts, trends, and emerging issues.* (3rd ed). Retrieved from http://www.naeyc.org/yc/pastissues/2014/november

Davis, J. (2010). *The first-generation college student experience.* Sterling, VA: Stylus Publishing.

Davis, D.M., & Hayes, J.A. (2012). What are the benefits of mindfulness? *American Psychological Association.* http://www.apa.org/monitor/2012/07-08/ce-corner.aspx.

Elias, M.J. (2004). The connection between social-emotional learning and learning disabilities:

Implications for intervention. *Learning Disability Quarterly* v27, 53-63. DOI:10.2307/1593632

Erikson, E. (1994). *Identity and the life cycle.* New York, NY: W.W. Norton.

Eye to Eye. (2017). *About Us.* Retrieved from http://eyetoeyenational.org/about/about.html

Gentry, J.H., & Campbell, M. (2002). Developing adolescents: A reference for professionals. Washington, D.C.: *The American Psychological Association.*

Goldberg, R.L. *The transition to college for Students with LD and AD/HD: The consultant's role.* Retrieved from www.iecaonline.com/pdf/IECA_Transition_to_College_for_LD_Students.pdf

Goldfus, M. (2015). *College students with LD/ADHD share what they've learned.* Retrieved from www.noodle.com/articles/college-students-with-ldadhd-share-their-dos-and-don'ts

Gorman, J.C. (2015). *Understanding children's hearts and minds: Emotional functioning and learning disabilities.* http://www.ldonline.org/article/6292/?theme=print.

Grigal, M., & Hart, D. (2010). *Think college: Postsecondary education options for students with intellectual disabilities.* Baltimore, MD: Paul H. Brookes Publishing Company.

Hadley, W.M. (2007). *The necessity of academic accommodations for first-year college students with learning disabilities.* Retrieved from www.nacacnet.org.

Institute of Educational Sciences National Center for Special Education Research. (2011). *The post-high school outcomes of young adults with disabilities up to 8 years after high school.* Nlts2.org/reports/2011_09_02/nlts2_report_2011_09_02_complete.pdf.

Kadison, R., & DiGeronimo, T.F. (2005). *College of the overwhelmed: The campus mental health crisis and what to do about it.* San Francisco, CA: Jossey-Bass.

Keng, S., Smoski, M.J., & Robins, C.J. (2011). Effects of mindfulness on psychological health: A review of empirical studies. *Clinical Psychology Review,* 31(6), 1041-1056. Retrieved from https://www.ncbi.nlm.nih.gov/pubmed/21802619

Kuther, T.L. (2016). *Socioemotional development in adolescence.* Retrieved from http://edge.sagepub.com/sites/default/files/12_KUTHER.pdf

Larose, S., Bernier, A., & Tarabulsy, G.M. (2005). Attachment state of mind, learning dispositions, and academic performance during the college transition. *Developmental Psychology,* 41, 281-289. Retrieved from https://www.ncbi.nlm.nih.gov/pubmed/15656755

Laursen, B., & Collins, W.A. (Eds.). (2012). *Relationship pathways: From adolescence to young adulthood.* Thousand Oaks, CA: Sage.

LDonline.org. (2017). *Students with disabilities advocate best for themselves.* Retrieved from http://www.ldonline.org/article/Students_with_Disabilities_Advocate_Best_for_Themselves

Lowe, K., & Dotterer, A.M. (2017). *Parental involvement during the college transition: A review and suggestion for its conceptual definition.* Retrieved from http://www.readcube.com/articles/10.1007/s40894-017-0058-z

Marklein, M.B. (2011). *Learning disabled students get a firmer grip on college.* USAtoday.com/news/education/story/2011-10-17/college-and-learning-disabilities.

Moore, R. (2015). *Making the jump: How to successfully transition from high school to college.* Nashville, TN: ClearVision Publishing.

Murray, C., Goldstein, D.E., Nourse, S., & Edgar, E. (2000). The postsecondary school attendance and completion rates of high school graduates with learning disabilities. *Learning Disabilities*

Research and Practice, 15 (3), 119-127. Retrieved from https://eric.ed.gov/?id=EJ612952

Roffman, A. (2007). *Guiding teens with learning disabilities: Navigating the transition from high school to adulthood.* New York, NY: The Princeton Review.

Shaw, S.F., Madaus, J.W., & Dukes, L.L. (2010). *Preparing students with disabilities for college success: A practical guide to transition planning.* Baltimore, MD: Paul H. Brookes Publishing Company.

Shek, D.T.L., & Wong, K.K. (2011). Do adolescent developmental issues disappear overnight? Reflections about holistic development in university students. *The Scientific World Journal,* 11, 353-361. Retrieved from https://www.ncbi.nlm.nih.gov/pubmed/21336451

Smith, C. (2011). *Lost in transition: The dark side of emerging adulthood.* New York, NY: Oxford University Press.

Spady, W.G. (1970). *Dropouts from higher education: An introductory review and synthesis. Interchange,* I, 64-85. Retrieved from https://eric.ed.gov/?id=EJ024800

Tanner, J. (2006). Recentering during emerging adulthood: A critical turning point in life span human development. In J.J. Arnett & J.L.Tanner (Eds.). *Emerging adults in America: Coming of age in the 21st century.* Washington, D.C.: APA.

Tinto, V. (1993). *Leaving college: Rethinking the causes and cures of student attrition.* Chicago, IL: University of Chicago Press.

Wessel, R.D., Jones, J.A., Markle, L., & Westfall, C. (2009). Retention and graduation of students with disabilities. *Journal of Postsecondary Education and Disabilities.* v.21 (3), 116-125. Retrieved from https://eric.ed.gov/?id=EJ831430

About the Primary Authors

Nicholas D. Young, PhD, EdD

Dr. Nicholas D. Young has worked in diverse educational roles for more than 28 years, serving as a principal, special education director, graduate professor, graduate program director, graduate dean, and longtime superintendent of schools. He was named the Massachusetts Superintendent of the Year; and he completed a distinguished Fulbright program focused on the Japanese educational system through the collegiate level. Dr. Young is the recipient of numerous other honors and recognitions including the General Douglas MacArthur Award for distinguished civilian and military leadership and the Vice Admiral John T. Hayward Award for exemplary scholarship. He holds several graduate degrees including a PhD in educational administration and an EdD in educational psychology.

Dr. Young has served in the U.S. Army and U.S. Army Reserves combined for over 33 years; and he graduated with distinction from the U.S. Air War College, the U.S. Army War College, and the U.S. Navy War College. After completing a series of senior leadership assignments in the U.S. Army Reserves as the commanding officer of the 287th Medical Company (DS), the 405th Area Support Company (DS), the 405th Combat Support Hospital, and the 399 Combat Support Hospital, he transitioned to his current military position as a faculty instructor at the U.S. Army War College in Carlisle, PA. He currently holds the rank of Colonel.

Dr. Young is also a regular presenter at state, national, and international conferences; and has written many books, book chapters, and/or articles on various topics in education, counseling, and psychology. Some of his most recent books include *Wrestling with Writing: Effective Strategies for Struggling Students* (in press); *From Lecture Hall to Laptop: Opportunities, Challenges, and the Continuing Evolution of Virtual Learning in Higher Education* (2017); *The Power of the Professoriate: Demands, Challenges, and Opportunities in 21st Century Higher Education* (2017); *To Campus with Confidence: Supporting the Successful Transition to College for Students with Learning Disabilities* (2017), *Paving the Pathway for*

Educational Success: Effective Classroom Interventions for Students with Learning Disabilities (in-press) *Floundering to Fluent: Reaching and Teaching the Struggling Student* (in-press); *Educational Entrepreneurship: Promoting Public-Private Partnerships for the 21st Century* (2015), *Beyond the Bedtime Story: Promoting Reading Development during the Middle School Years* (2015), *Betwixt and Between: Understanding and Meeting the Social and Emotional Developmental Needs of Students During the Middle School Transition Years* (2014), *Learning Style Perspectives: Impact Upon the Classroom* (3rd ed., 2014); and *Collapsing Educational Boundaries from Preschool to PhD: Building Bridges Across the Educational Spectrum* (2013), *Transforming Special Education Practices: A Primer for School Administrators and Policy Makers* (2012), and *Powerful Partners in Student Success: Schools, Families and Communities* (2012). He also co-authored several children's books to include the popular series *I am Full of Possibilities*. Dr. Young may be contacted directly at nyoung1191@aol.com.

Christine N. Michael, PhD

Dr. Christine N. Michael is a more than 40-year educational veteran with a variety of professional experiences. She holds degrees from Brown University, Rhode Island College, Union Institute and University, and the University of Connecticut, where she earned a PhD in education, human development, and family relations. Her previous work has included middle and high school teaching, higher education administration, college teaching, and educational consulting. She has also been involved with Head Start, Upward Bound, national non-profits Foundation for Excellent Schools and College for Every Student, and the federal Trio programs, and has published widely on topics in education and psychology. Her most recent works included serving as a primary author on the book *To Campus with Confidence: Supporting the Successful Transition to College for Students with Learning Disabilities* (2017), *Beyond the Bedtime Story: Promoting Reading Development during the Middle School Years* (2015), *Betwixt and Between: Understanding and Meeting the Social and Emotional Development Needs of Students During the Middle School Transition Years* (2014), and *Powerful Partners in Student Success: Schools, Families and Communities* (2012). She is currently the Program Director of Low Residency Programs at American International College. Dr. Michael may be contacted at cnevadam@gmail.com.

Teresa Allissa Citro, PhD

Dr. Teresa Allissa Citro is the Chief Executive Officer, Learning Disabilities Worldwide, Inc. and the Founder and President of Thread of Hope, Inc., Dr. Citro is a graduate of Tufts New England Medical School and Northeastern University, Boston. She has co-edited several books on a wide range of topics in special education and has co-authored a popular children's series *I Am Full of Possibilities.* Furthermore, Dr. Citro is the co-editor of two peer review journals *including Learning Disabilities: A Contemporary Journal* and *Insights on Learning Disabilities from Prevailing Theories to Validated Practices.* She is the mother of two young children and resides in Boston, Massachusetts.

CPSIA information can be obtained
at www.ICGtesting.com
Printed in the USA
BVOW10*0438301117
501335BV00011B/144/P